M000287599

World of Reading

**A Thematic Approach
to Reading Comprehension**

2

TEACHER'S MANUAL
with TESTS and ANSWER KEYS

Joan Baker-González
University of Puerto Rico, Mayagüez (retired)

Eileen K. Blau
University of Puerto Rico, Mayagüez

PEARSON
Longman

World of Reading 2
A Thematic Approach to Reading Comprehension
Teacher's Manual with Tests and Answer Keys

Copyright © 2010 by Pearson Education, Inc.
All rights reserved.

No part of this publication may be reproduced, stored in a retrieval system, or transmitted in any form or by any means, electronic, mechanical, photocopying, recording, or otherwise, without the prior permission of the publisher.

Pearson Education, 10 Bank Street, White Plains, NY 10606

Staff Credits: Pietro Alongi, Rhea Banker, Mindy DePalma, Dave Dickey, Christine Edmonds, Oliva Fernandez, Gosia Janos-White, Chris Leonowicz, Martha McGaughey, Linda Moser, Paula Van Ells, and Pat Wosczyk

Cover design: Pat Wosczyk
Text composition: ElectraGraphics, Inc.
Text font: 11/13 Times
Text design: Ann France

Text Credits: **Page 78** "Dealing with Peer Pressure" reprinted with permission from www.kidshealth.org. Copyright © 1995–2008. Nemours Foundation/KidsHealth. **Page 83** "People on the Move: Moving Young," from *State of the World Population 2006*, www.unfpa.org. **Page 87** Adapted with permission from "Robots Set to Overhaul Service Industry" by Tom A. Peter, from the February 25, 2008 issue of the *Christian Science Monitor* (www.csmonitor.com).© 2008 the *Christian Science Monitor*. All rights reserved. **Page 92** "Will You Go Out with Me?" by Laura Ullman. **Page 96** "A Frightening Deadline" by Malcolm McConnell from "They Dared to Dream," reprinted with permission from *Reader's Digest*. Copyright © 1996 by The Reader's Digest Association, Inc. **Page 101** Copyright © by Isaac Asimov. Reprinted by permission of the Estate of Isaac Asimov.

ISBN-13: 978-0-13-600212-3
ISBN-10: 0-13-600212-9

PEARSON LONGMAN ON THE **WEB**

Pearsonlongman.com offers online resources for teachers and students. Access our Companion Websites, our online catalog, and our local offices around the world.

Visit us at **pearsonlongman.com**.

Printed in the United States of America
3 4 5 6 7 8 9 10—OPM—13 12 11 10 09

CONTENTS

Chapter-By-Chapter Teaching Tips

Welcome to the Teacher's Manual for *World of Reading 2*

World of Reading has been designed to enable students to read authentic materials written for adult native speakers of English. The primary difficulty students have in reading authentic material is with vocabulary. Of course, knowing the meanings of words and expressions does not guarantee better reading comprehension, as there is a number of other important factors involved. However, the number of words needed to comprehend authentic material for adults presents a considerable hurdle.[1] Getting over this hurdle requires work and dedication on the part of students; one important role for teachers is to support their students in this undertaking. Two ways teachers can do this are to: 1) provide consistent and repeated exposure to target words and expressions students need to learn (i.e., recycle vocabulary), and 2) help students deepen their knowledge of words by learning multiple meanings for words in a variety of contexts.

Many of the tips in Part One of the *Teacher's Manual* will help you with these two tasks. First, the Recycling Vocabulary section lists vocabulary targeted in earlier readings and also provides the earlier context so you do not have to look for it. Second, exercise models give additional exposure to target words and expressions in meaningful ways. Finally, there are occasional suggestions of ways that you can help students remember the meanings of words by understanding something about their construction or etymology. In addition to helping develop students' vocabularies, the tips also provide ways to improve students' understanding of text organization and other text features.

Recall that in the Teacher's Introduction to the Student Book, you will find a full description of the series, including suggestions for how to handle different exercises. At the back of the book, there is a chapter-by-chapter list of targeted vocabulary, which should be useful in planning review activities and writing quizzes and exams. Words included in that list are targeted in one of three ways: 1) They are pre-taught at some point before reading (Unit Opener, About the Reading, Thinking about the Topic, Previewing), 2) They are included in marginal multiple-choice exercises, or 3) They are incorporated into the Vocabulary section, either in Vocabulary Building or in the second, more specialized exercise.

Part One of the Teacher's Manual (Chapter-by-Chapter Teaching Tips) is followed by the student book answer key and unit tests and test answer keys.

---

[1] It is estimated that a person needs a vocabulary of at least 3,000–5,000 word families to begin to read authentic academic materials. (Nation, Paul and Waring, Robert. [1997] Vocabulary size, text coverage and word lists. In Schmitt, Norbert and McCarthy, Michael, eds. "Vocabulary-Description, Acquisition and Pedagogy" pp. 6–19. Cambridge University Press.) The estimate is more like 10,000 to do university work in English with reasonable ease. (Hazenberg, S. & Hulstijn, J. [1996]. Defining a minimal receptive second-language vocabulary for non-native university students: An empirical investigation. *Applied Linguistics* 17(2), 145–163.)

Chapter-by-Chapter Teaching Tips

Unit Opener *(page 1)*

As students discuss the questions and quote, you can write words related to the unit topic on the board, either those that students use correctly in the discussion or those that they need to learn. After the discussion, have students pronounce any new words and check to see that their meaning is clear. Offer definitions and example sentences as needed. Students will probably know most vocabulary needed to discuss the questions, but you might improve the discussion by teaching students words and expressions such as: *love from parents or caretakers, a decent place to live, stability, having responsibilities, peer pressure, parental pressure, parents' expectations, teachers' expectations, money worries.*

CHAPTER 1
My Early Memories

Previewing *(page 2)*

After completing the exercise, you may want to tell students that many paragraphs begin with a sentence that clarifies the topic (what the paragraph is about). Therefore, it is a good previewing technique to read the first sentence of each paragraph to get an idea of what topics the reading covers.

Read *(page 3)*

If students used *World of Reading 1,* ask them if they remember the following vocabulary items: *apparently* (as it appears/seems), *behavior, give up* (stop trying), *pressure* (blood pressure, pressure builds in rocks before an earthquake), *secure* (fasten or make tight). Call on volunteers to explain the meanings or, if necessary, provide them yourself. Tell students they will see these items in the reading, but perhaps with new meanings.

You may want to use the word *slow* to distinguish between a literal meaning (physically slow) and a figurative meaning (mentally slow, not too smart).

The word *jock* is an informal and often disapproving word for an athlete, suggesting that the person is not intelligent.

The word *kin* is an old word for family or relatives, as in *next of kin; kinfolk* is still heard in parts of the U.S. today.

Vocabulary

Recall that paragraph 1 of the reading was done in the Student's Introductory Chapter. The vocabulary help for paragraph 1 is there.

Vocabulary Building (page 5)

Item 1, *aimless*: Demonstrating the meaning of words is often more successful than giving verbal definitions. Write *aim* + *less* on the board. Demonstrate the meaning of *aim* by pointing an imaginary gun at a clock, window, or door in the room. Ask students what the suffix *-less* means *(without)*; *aimless* means without direction, or a sense of knowing where you are going.

Though it is not target vocabulary, you can also demonstrate *swing* and *a miss* if students are not familiar with that baseball expression.

Item 3, *humiliate*: It might help students remember the meaning of the word *humiliation* (and the verb *humiliate*) if you connect it to the word *humble* (feeling small and unimportant).

Phrasal Verbs

Call students' attention to the phrases *gave up* (Item 7) and *looked out for* (Item 12) on page 5. Tell students that these multiword expressions are called phrasal verbs. Point out that, in order to read English well, students need to recognize phrasal verbs as meaningful units.

General Information: Phrasal Verbs

Phrasal verbs consist of two (and sometimes three) words: a verb that is followed by a particle such as *on, off, out,* or *up*. The meaning of some phrasal verbs is quite literal and easy to see; others are idiomatic, and students will need to know how to find them in their dictionaries. In some learner dictionaries (such as *Longman Dictionary of American English*), phrasal verbs follow the entry for the verb, are printed in boldface, and followed by *phr. v.* Phrasal verbs, like other verbs, can have more than one meaning; some are slang, most are rather informal, but some can be fairly formal.

Phrasal verbs are a productive category in contemporary English. Ask students to give examples that they use frequently, for example, *turn on, turn off, chill out,* and *hang out,* among many others.

Phrasal verbs are an important aspect of English. Those that are not in exercises are listed in the Vocabulary Reminder List so that you can easily check that students see them as units of meaning. You can ask questions that require students to use the phrasal verbs, both the verb and its particle, in their answers, for example: *What did the runner do?* (She *put* on her shoes) or *What is the verb in this sentence?* (put on) Be sure students mention the verb and the particle.

Handling Non-essential Vocabulary (page 6)

This exercise shows students that, when reading authentic material containing many words they do not know, it is a good idea to learn to skip non-essential words, at least on the first reading. They can, however, infer at least partial meaning for many non-essential words if they make the effort to do so.

Vocabulary Review (page 7)

Scolding was targeted in the Student's Introductory Chapter. You might help students remember the word by asking them if they remember getting a scolding when they were younger. They might enjoy sharing stories about what they did wrong and what a parent or caretaker said or did about the misbehavior.

Vocabulary Reminder List

The Vocabulary Reminder List section reminds you of things you can show students about vocabulary in the readings, including phrasal verbs, collocations, verbs and adjectives + the prepositions they require, synonyms and antonyms, and words for analysis.

Collocations

Collocations are words that native speakers often use together. For a more complete discussion of them, see comments for Collocations in the Unit Wrap-Up for Unit 2. Following is a list of collocations from this chapter: *do two things at the same time* (¶1), *escape hatch* (¶2), *have a bad day* (¶3).

CHAPTER 2

Peer Influences on Achievement

Thinking about the Topic (page 9)

Tell students that the words *pressure, influence, behavior,* and *adolescence* are in italics because they are defined in this section; they are target vocabulary words—ones students need to learn. Ask them to find the definitions. Note that students must understand what *influence* and *behavior* mean before they can read the definition of *put pressure on.*

Comprehension Check (page 11)

This article is the first opportunity to help students understand how research is planned. After doing the Comprehension Check, Second Reading, you might want to have students summarize the essential facts about the research in a diagram. For example:

BEGINNING OF THE STUDY	END OF THE STUDY (3 YEARS LATER)
Group A—students with more academically-oriented friends	had better grades
Group B—students with less academically-oriented friends	had lower grades
Group C—students with friends who had more behavior problems	had more behavior problems
Group D—students with friends with fewer behavior problems	had fewer behavior problems

Vocabulary

Vocabulary Building *(page 12)*

Item 1, *academic*: It might help students remember the meaning of the word *academic* if they know that an academy is a type of school.

Item 2, *equivalent*: The word *equivalent* is used here to mean "of similar value," not exactly the same.

Item 8, *alienated*: Knowing that an alien is a foreigner or creature from outer space may help students remember that the word *alienated* means "outside the group."

Some students are unclear about when to use adjectives and when to use adverbs. Note the opportunity here to distinguish *academic* from *academically*. The adjective precedes a noun (academic career) and the adverb precedes an adjective (academically oriented). You could also write the sentence *They did well _____*, on the board and ask which word fills the blank.

Identifying Essential and Non-essential Vocabulary *(page 12)*

You might want to ask students to try to infer partial meaning of the non-essential words: *period* (length of time), *sorts of* (kinds of), *profile* (a picture of behavior), *legitimate* (possibly *good*). Thinking about the vocabulary's meaning, even if students get only a general idea, will make it more likely that the next time they see the word, they will understand it.

Vocabulary Review *(page 13)*

The Vocabulary Review exercise contains two words that can function as either verbs or nouns without adding a suffix, *crowd* and *conduct*; another is *track*. As a noun, *track* means a place to run (*running track*) or where a train runs (*railroad track*). As a verb, it means to follow what happens to something or somebody. Ask students if they can give other examples of words that can be both nouns and verbs without a change in form. You can also use this exercise using words from the reading.

Circle N if the underlined word is being used as a noun and V if a verb.

1. How much <u>time</u> do you spend on homework?   Ⓝ   V
   Who is going to <u>time</u> the runners?   N   Ⓥ
2.*It is not easy to <u>conduct</u> a long-term research project.   N   Ⓥ
   The students whose <u>conduct</u> was good tended to have friends
   who behaved well.   Ⓝ   V
3. The students <u>crowd</u> into the cafeteria at lunchtime every day.   N   Ⓥ
   The <u>crowd</u> you hang out with in high school is important.   Ⓝ   V
4. The research showed that friends <u>influence</u> academic performance.   N   Ⓥ
   Friends have a lot of <u>influence</u> on young people.   Ⓝ   V
5.*We are looking for <u>contrasts</u> between the two groups.   Ⓝ   V
   The research report <u>contrasts</u> successful and unsuccessful students.   N   Ⓥ

*Note that when *conduct* and *contrast* are verbs, the primary stress is on the second syllable; when they are nouns, the stress is on the first syllable. Remind students that if they look up a word under the wrong part of speech, they will get incorrect meanings.

Vocabulary Reminder List

Collocations: *change over time* (¶1), *get in(to) trouble* (¶3), *all other things being equal* (¶3), *long-term . . . plans* (¶4), *day-to-day* (¶4)

Read *(page 15)*

If students used *World of Reading 1*, ask them if they remember the following vocabulary items: *find out* (learn), *ignore* (not pay attention to), *tease* (make fun of). Call on volunteers to explain the meanings or provide them, if necessary. Tell students they will see these items in the reading, but they might have new meanings.

Vocabulary

Vocabulary Building: Synonyms *(page 18)*

This is the first of several synonym exercises in the book. Knowledge of synonyms is an important part of the foundation for writing. Students need to know more than one way to say something in order to paraphrase ideas and avoid plagiarism, and also to add variety to their writing. It is not recommended that pairs of synonyms or antonyms be presented for the first time together. However, once students are familiar with both words, they can practice them together.

It is best to think of synonyms as words with similar meanings, not the same meaning. They often differ in level of formality (register), positive or negative associations in most people's minds (connotation), and the words they combine with (collocation). You can illustrate this with some of the words in this vocabulary building exercise.

Item 1, *mean*: *mean* sounds quite negative; it is closer to *cruel* than it is to *unkind*.

Item 2, *minor*: *not serious* is a better synonym for *minor* in a medical context because all health matters are important to a person. In other contexts, *not very important* is a perfectly good synonym.

Item 3, *bother*: *bother* is a common word, as is *upset*. *Disturb* is more formal and has some specific collocations such as *disturb someone's sleep, disturb the peace*.

Item 4, *toddler*: Both *little kid* and *preschooler* are good synonyms for *toddler*, but they do not convey the specific image that *toddler* does. Ask students how children about 1–2 years old walk. That kind of walk is 'toddling,' hence children 1–3 years old are called *toddlers*.

Item 5, *comment*: In this context, *talk about* is closer in meaning to *comment* than *mention*.

Item 6, *weird*: Both b and c are good synonyms. However, *weird* has its own connotation, usually negative. It is also informal.

Item 7, *awkward*: *uncomfortable* is closer in meaning to *awkward* in this context; *embarrassed* suggests a stronger uncomfortable feeling, one that comes from looking foolish in front of other people.

Item 8, *presume*: *presume* is more formal than either *suppose* or *think*.

Item 9, *am capable of doing*: *Be capable of* sounds more formal than either *can* or *be able to*.

Synonyms and antonyms will be called to your attention in the Vocabulary Reminder List.

Multiword Expressions *(page 19)*

> ## General Information: Multiword Expressions
>
> Multiword Expression (MWE) is a general cover term for a variety of word groups or lexical phrases where meaning is associated with a phrase, not a single word. MWEs include:
>
> | | |
> |---|---|
> | phrasal verbs | *find out* (learn) and *put up with* (tolerate) |
> | collocations | *more than anyone could ever imagine* and *It's all right to be* _____ |
> | verb or adjective + preposition | *think about, afraid of* |
> | Idioms, proverbs, and sayings | *get out of hand, get a kick out of, Rome wasn't built in a day.* |

It is important for students to learn MWEs as units. Learning meaningful language chunks focuses students' attention on English, instead of translating word for word from their native language. It helps them sound more like native speakers, read more efficiently, and gain fluency.

Learners do not necessarily recognize chunks of meaningful language when they hear or see them. For this reason, MWEs not in specific exercises are listed in the Vocabulary Reminder List in the *Teacher's Manual.* If you prepare practices like the matching exercise below, you will encourage students to pay attention to which words go together.

Match the words on the left with the best choice on the right to form a collocation (words that go together). You will not use all the choices. Use a match only once.

    _____ 1. Angie learned to stick up   a. oriented.

    _____ 2. Powell's family cared   b. for herself.

    _____ 3. My sister studies a lot; she is academically-   c. delinquent.

    _____ 4. That guy is no good. Stay away   d. about him.

                                                   e. from him.

(Answers: 1. b, 2. d, 3. a, 4. e)

The exercise above can be given to students in abbreviated form without the context. For example:

    _____ 1. stick up   a. oriented

    _____ 2. care   b. for yourself

    _____ 3. academically   c. delinquent

    _____ 4. stay away   d. about him

                                         e. from him

The more context you give, the more the focus is on total meaning rather than just recognizing the words that go together; both types of practice can be valuable.

Vocabulary Reminder List

Phrasal verbs: *worked out* (¶6) is a variant of *figured out* = decided

Antonyms: *major/minor*

Text Analysis *(page 20)*

You may want to extend this exercise by reviewing the usual purposes for introductions and conclusions listed below and asking students to comment on the purpose of the introduction and conclusion to this reading.

An introduction usually

- gets the reader's interest

- states the topic

- states or suggests the writer's purpose for writing

- states or suggests the main idea

A conclusion usually

- provides a closing, or completion, to the article.

- summarizes or reviews important ideas in the body.

CHAPTER 4
To a Daughter Leaving Home

Read *(page 22)*

Poetry is meant to be heard, so either you or one of your students should read this poem aloud. You might ask students to read the poem silently first, imagining how it should sound if read aloud.

Then ask students where they think they should pause as they read the poem. Note that, although Pastan uses several commas where the reader needs to pause slightly, she uses only one period. Ask students if they note any effect from the poem being one long sentence *(possibly a sense that the girl on the bicycle is rapidly getting farther and farther away from her parent or that when you learn to ride a bicycle you must keep going or you fall off)*.

Text Analysis *(page 24)*

After seeing the effect of the simile (hair flapping behind you like a handkerchief waving goodbye) and the metaphor (growing up is compared to learning to ride a bicycle) in this poem, students might enjoy trying to write some similes and metaphors of their own. Offer students some ideas to help them begin. For example, suggest the simile frame, *My dog looks like / runs like / smiles like . . .* or *My dog is as hyper as a . . .*

It is more difficult to write original metaphors, but these sentences may give students some ideas:

Right now our school is a volcano waiting to explode.

Why is the campus such a garbage dump?

My sister is a real pain.

Linking Readings

Once you complete Unit 1, you might want to use these questions for discssion: 1. What connections can you make between the research on peer pressure and the kind of pressure Angie faced? 2. What does each reading suggest are different kinds of pressure children face when growing up? 3. What does each reading suggest are important issues in early childhood and adolescence? Accept all responses as long as students can support them with examples and information from the unit.

Unit Wrap-Up

Word Families *(page 25)*

Parts of Speech

If students have not used *World of Reading 1*, you may need to check that they can recognize the four major parts of speech.

> **General Information: Parts of Speech**
>
> **Nouns** give the name of a person, place, thing, or abstract concept; they answer the questions *Who?* or *What?* Most nouns follow articles (a *box*, an *elephant*, the *newspaper*, some *butter*) possessive forms (my *money*, his *children*, their *house*) and quantifier questions (How much *coffee?* How many *cups?*)
>
> **Verbs** refer to an action (*run*), mental activity (*think*), or state of being (*be, have*). In English, verbs change form when referring to now, every day, yesterday, and tomorrow (*am walking* now, *walk* every day, *walked* yesterday, *am going to walk* tomorrow). Verbs can be used after modals and the auxiliary verbs *be* and *have* (will *go*, should *try*, am *running*, have *seen*). *To* + base verb gives the infinitive form (I like *to run*.).
>
> **Adjectives** come before nouns (*red* sunset) and follow verbs like *be, seem, look,* and *appear*. (She *seems* happy.) They often follow *very* and other intensifiers like *quite, really,* and *extremely*. (It is *extremely* cold today.) They answer the question *What kind of?* For example, a *hilarious* movie; the movie was *hilarious.*
>
> **Adverbs** of manner commonly end in *-ly*. (*quickly, intensely*) Many adverbs (also called adverbials) are not single words, but phrases like *in the morning, at the park,* and *every day*. Adverbs and adverbial phrases answer these questions about the verb: *How?* (walk *quickly*); *Where?* (walk *to the store*); *When?* (walk *in the morning*); *How often?* (walk *every day*); and *Why?* (walk *for exercise*).

The following exercise will allow you to check that students recognize parts of speech without asking them to explain how they know.

Circle the function of the nonsense word SMOTCH for each sentence.

1.	We SMOTCH every day.	N	(V)	Adj	Adv
2.	He's a very SMOTCH teacher.	N	V	(Adj)	Adv
3.	They want to SMOTCH the house.	N	(V)	Adj	Adv
4.	We saw the big SMOTCH.	(N)	V	Adj	Adv
5.	He talks very SMOTCHLY.	N	V	Adj	(Adj)
6.	I can't SMOTCH with you today.	N	(V)	Adj	Adv
7.	They seem very SMOTCH.	N	V	(Adj)	Adv
8.	Do you have any SMOTCHES?	(N)	V	Adj	Adv

After students have studied the Word Families chart and completed the exercise, ask them to find suffixes that mark each of the four parts of speech:

Nouns: *-ment, -tion/-ation,* and *-ance/-ence.*

Verbs: *-ate, -yze/-ize*

Adjectives: *-ic, -ical, -ent, -tial, -ed,* and *-ing*

Adverbs: *-ly*

Ask students for examples of other words that use these suffixes. Mention that a few adjectives end in *-ly* (*friendly, lovely, likely*)

General Information: Shifting Primary Stress

Correct location of the primary stress on a word is critically important to a native speaker's understanding the word. For example, if the word *control* is pronounced CONtrol, rather than conTROL, it is likely a native speaker will have trouble understanding. The following words in the Word Families in Unit 1 show a shift in primary stress:

aCAdemy	acaDEMic (-ally)
Alien	alieNAtion
ANalyze	anaLYtical (-ally)
humiliAtion	huMIliate (huMIliated)
INfluence	influENtial
TRAUma	trauMAtic

Go over the chart with students, checking their pronunciation of the words. The exercise in the Word Families section of the Unit Wrap-Up uses only one or two of the words in each row of the chart. Time permitting, have students use some of the other words in oral or written sentences.

Words With More Than One Meaning *(page 26)*

To help students learn multiple meanings of these words, have them make word bank cards that illustrate the different meanings they will need most.

For example, write on the board:

awkward   1. uncomfortable

2. moving/behaving in a way that doesn't seem relaxed or comfortable

Students can use sentences from the reading, example sentences from the *Longman Dictionary of American English*, or original sentences if you have time to check the accuracy of the students' work.

If students write original sentences, show them how to give enough context in their sentences to demonstrate that they know the meanings of the word. For example:

- I was in an awkward situation. (Unacceptable: The sentence does not show what *awkward* means; it could just as well mean "pleasant" as "uncomfortable.")

- I was in an awkward situation when my friend found out that I didn't tell him the complete truth. (Acceptable: The sentence gives enough context to show that "awkward" means something "difficult.")

Recommended Readings

Cisneros, Sandra. "Eleven" and "Mexican Movies." *Woman Hollering Creek and other stories.* New York: Vintage Books, 1991.

> Two very short stories about growing up. The first deals with a child's sensitivity at the age of eleven; the second deals with the security children get from their parents.

Ehrlich, Amy. *When I Was Your Age, Volume One: Original Stories about Growing Up.* Cambridge: Candlewick Press, (Ed.) 2001.

Ortiz Cofer, Judith. "The Game." *The Latin Deli.* Norton, W. W. & Company, Inc. 1995.

> A poem about a child growing up with a physical deformity.

UNIT 2 BETWEEN TWO WORLDS

Unit Opener *(page 28)*

As students discuss the questions and quote, you can write words related to the unit topic on the board, either those that the students use correctly in the discussion or those that they need to learn. After the discussion, have students pronounce any new words and check to see that their meaning is clear. Offer definitions and example sentences as needed. Students will probably know most vocabulary needed to discuss the questions, but you might improve the discussion by teaching students words and expressions such as: *unemployment at home, better opportunities abroad, to escape violence, war, poverty, persecution, new customs/laws/jobs, do needed jobs, do jobs others don't want, start businesses.*

The quote gives you an opportunity to review the concept of metaphor from Chapter 4. Ask students to find a metaphor in this poem *(an immigrant is a door)* and to explain how an immigrant and a door are similar.

CHAPTER 5
People on the Move: Moving Young

Read *(page 30)*

Recycling Vocabulary

If students used *World of Reading 1,* ask them if they remember the following vocabulary items: *obstacle* (something blocking your way), *destination* (a place you are going), *huge* (big). Call on volunteers to explain the meanings or, if necessary, provide them yourself. Tell students they will see these items in the reading, but perhaps with new meanings.

The chart below lists vocabulary items from this chapter that have also appeared in earlier chapters of this book. There are several ways you can use this information.

- Put the words in the left column on the board and tell students they will see them in the new reading, sometimes with a new meaning. Ask students if they remember the word or a related word from an earlier reading. Add these words in the right column.

- For the words that vary in form, ask students what part of speech each is. For example, say, "In Chapter 1 we saw the word *destined*. What kind of word is it? (*adjective*) In this reading, we will see *destination*. What kind of word is it? (*noun*)."

- Ask students to give example sentences using the words.

- When appropriate, ask about the parts of the word, as in *destination* (*destin* – base + *-ation* – noun suffix)

- Alternatively, you may want to point these words out after a first reading.

LOCATION IN CHAPTER 5	LOCATION IN EARLIER CHAPTER(S)
destination (¶2)	*destined:* "Marilyn was destined for college." (Chapter 1)
lack (¶3)	*lacked:* "lacked drive" (Chapter 1)

Comprehension Check

Second Reading *(page 31)*

Tell students that the questions in this exercise are intended to help them learn how to highlight or take notes by suggesting what is important. Talk with students about what they do to remember important ideas and information that they read for classes. What are the disadvantages of not taking notes or highlighting information? What do good highlighting and note-taking skills require? *(the ability to distinguish between important and less important ideas and information)* Clarify that it makes no sense to copy everything, and if nearly everything is highlighted, the highlighting is not useful.

Vocabulary

Vocabulary Building *(page 32)*

Remind students of the usefulness of recognizing meaningful parts of words. Ask students to find two suffixes that mark nouns. The suffix *-ness* changes adjectives into nouns (*resourcefulness*—Item 2) and *-ism* changes nouns into other nouns that have a variety of meanings, including belief (*racism*—Item 11). Ask students to suggest other nouns that end in these suffixes such as: *goodness, kindness, greatness, sickness, vegetarianism, criticism,* and *heroism.* The parts of the word *xenophobia* (Item 12) are *xeno-* which comes from a Greek word meaning 'guest or foreigner,' and the word *phobia* which means fear, also from Greek.

Using a Dictionary *(page 33)*

General Information: Using a Dictionary

Check that students can interpret the way the dictionary presents information. Ask them how separate meanings are marked. *(boldfaced numbers)* Ask how example sentences are marked. *(italics)*

Using the dictionary entries on pp. 33–34 in the Student Book, point out other things that users can learn from dictionary entries, such as:

- Pronunciation and primary stress
- Part of speech (noun, verb, adjective, adverb)
- Whether nouns are countable (*C*) or uncountable (*U*)
- Parts of irregular verbs: *seek, sought, sought*
- Other members of a word family: *eagerly (adv)* and *eagerness (n)*
- Collocations in the examples: *eager to please*

Finally, remind students of the steps in using the dictionary correctly:

1. Read the sentence carefully to determine the part of speech of the word.
2. Find the entry for the appropriate part of speech in the dictionary.
3. Read the individual definitions and examples to find the one that makes sense in the context.
4. Look for phrasal verbs and other expressions in boldface after the entries for the main word.

Vocabulary Reminder List

Collocations: *set in motion* (¶1), *face obstacles* (¶2), *on the move* (¶3), *find a way* (¶3), *aging population* (¶5), *domestic work* (¶5), *There is a growing demand for . . .* (¶5)

Synonyms: *seek* (formal) = look for

Antonyms: *receiving / sending (countries)*

Verb + preposition: *integrate + into* (¶7), *protect (someone/something) from* (¶7), *depend on* (¶7)

Word analysis: *immigrant*: *im-* (in) + *migrant* (person who moves) = person who moves from one country into another (the [*n*] in *in-* becomes [*m*] before [*m*] in the root word); *emigrant* = e- (from) + *migrant* = a person who leaves his/her country.

Text Analysis *(page 35)*

This practice gives you another opportunity to review what successful introduction and conclusions do (see page 8 in this *Teacher's Manual*).

Read *(page 36)*

Recycling Vocabulary

If students used *World of Reading 1*, ask them if they remember the following vocabulary item: *drop out of* (school). Call on a volunteer to explain the meaning or, if necessary, provide it yourself. Tell students they will see this expression in the reading.

Refer to page 12 for ideas on how to review these words in meaningful activities.

LOCATION IN CHAPTER 6	LOCATION IN EARLIER CHAPTER(S)
concerned (¶6)	*concerned:* "Parents have reason to be concerned about the qualities of their children's friends." (Chapter 2)
get/be stuck (¶6) (participial adjective from the verb *stick* = glue; meaning unable to move)	*stuck:* Powell "stuck a hairpin in an outlet." (Chapter 1) (past tense of *stick* = put, push in)

The instructions in the student book ask students to read one of the parts and share what they learn with their classmates. You can use the following alternatives to approach these readings: students read one part in class and the other for homework; students read both parts and compare and contrast the lives of the two young women using a Venn Diagram.

If students are responsible for both readings, they will be ready for the Unit Test which tests, via cloze passages, two vocabulary items from each reading (*shortage, make ends meet, empowering,* and *enable*).

Vocabulary

Vocabulary Building *(page 41)*

Item 3 (Bibi), *vicious cycle*: It may help students remember the expression *vicious cycle* if they know the word *vice* (from *vice squad*—a police unit that deals with violent crimes; it can also mean a bad or dangerous habit). If so, relating *vicious* to *vice* should help them remember the meaning of *vicious* (*violent, dangerous,* or *cruel*).

Items 1 and 4 (Rajini), *empower* and *enable*: Ask students what the prefix *en- / em-* in *enable* and *empower* means (*make* or *give*).

Item 3 (Rajini), *make up for*: Remind students that a small difference in words makes a big difference in meaning (*make up for* = compensate for, but *make up* = stop fighting, become friends again; invent, imagine).

Item 6 (Rajini), *destiny*: Students may benefit from connecting *destiny* (what lies ahead of you in life) with *destination* (the end point of a trip).

Vocabulary Reminder List

Phrasal verbs: *get ahead* (¶6 Bibi) = make progress, especially financial; *come back* (¶6 Bibi) = return; *pay back* (¶3 Rajini) = return borrowed money; *deal with* (¶4 Rajini) = handle, manage

Collocations: *spend time* (¶1 Bibi), *There's no shortage of* (¶5 Bibi), *give-and-take* (¶6), *learn from experience* (¶1 Rajini), *the turning point* (¶2 Rajini)

Verb + preposition: *cover for* (¶4 Bibi) = do work that someone else is supposed to do; *cope with* (¶2 Rajini); *dream of/about* (¶3 Rajini)

Word analysis: *oversee: over-* (from above) + *see* = watch from a superior position, supervise. (*Supervise* has the same structure using Latin forms; *super* [above] + *vis* (see).)

Text Analysis *(page 43)*

You might want to call students' attention to the fact that the order of the causes and effects depends on the connector:

1. *so, therefore, as a result:*

      cause   connector   effect/result
   I couldn't sleep, *so* I cleaned the house.

   I couldn't sleep; *therefore* I cleaned the house.

   I couldn't sleep, *as a result,* I cleaned the house.

2. *because, since:*

   effect/result   connector   cause
   I cleaned the house *because* I couldn't sleep.

   I cleaned the house *since* I couldn't sleep.

CHAPTER 7

Bosnia's Loss is an American City's Gain

Read *(page 44)*

Recycling Vocabulary

If students used *World of Reading 1,* ask them if they remember the following vocabulary items: *concentrate/concentration* (focus attention/focused attention), *expect.* Call on volunteers to explain the meanings or provide them, if necessary. Tell students they will see these items in the reading, but they might have new meanings.

Refer to page 12 for ideas on how to review these words in meaningful activities.

LOCATION IN CHAPTER 7	LOCATION IN EARLIER CHAPTER
stuck (¶1)	*get/be stuck* (Chapter 6, ¶6 Bibi)
(participial adjective from the verb *stick* = glue; meaning 'not progressing')	(participial adjective from *stick* = glue; meaning 'unable to move')

Vocabulary

Vocabulary Building (page 48)

Item 7: The meaning of the word *proportionally* might be easier to remember if students see the word *portion* (a portion of food—the size of the serving) in it.

Vocabulary Reminder List

Phrasal verbs: *grew up* (¶2) = spent his childood/youth, *come in* = enter (¶2), *build* (place) *into* = transform(¶6)

Collocations: *sit on our hands* (¶2), *have a reputation for* (¶3), *lose its appeal* (¶6), *have an impact on* (¶15)

Synonyms: *aid* (¶9) = help, *landed* (¶9) = settled, *decline* (¶7) = decrease

Verb + preposition: *ask for* (¶2)

Word analysis: *upsurge* (¶9) *up* + *surge* (a sudden large increase in something) = sudden increase (Note that *surge* carries the bulk of the meaning.)

CHAPTER 8
(Un)American

Read (page 51)

Recycling Vocabulary

If students used *World of Reading 1*, ask them if they remember the following vocabulary item: *signal* (v. mean/communicate, n. sign). Call on a volunteer to explain the meaning or provide it, if necessary. Tell students they will see this word in the reading.

Refer to page 12 for ideas how to review these words in meaningful activities.

LOCATION IN CHAPTER 8	LOCATION IN EARLIER CHAPTER(S)
actually (¶1)	*actually:* "whether the types of friends adolescents have actually makes a difference." (Chapter 2)
weird (¶2)	*weird:* "They said I [Angie] talked really weird." (Chapter 3)

Vocabulary

Vocabulary Building (page 53)

Item 9, *transferred*: Use the word *transferred* to call students' attention to the prefix *trans-* (also in *transportation, transatlantic, transplant*). Explain that it is a Latin prefix meaning *across*. Knowing this prefix may help students remember that *transfer* means "move from one place to another" or "move across some space."

Vocabulary Reminder List

Collocations: *the latest gossip* (¶4), *tears streamed down her cheeks* (¶4), *I wonder if . . .* (¶6), *I didn't think it was funny.* (¶8)

Verb + preposition: *listen to* (¶5) (listen *to* music, not listen music)

Word analysis: *outsider* (¶2) outside + -*er* = person who is not part of the group

Text Analysis *(page 54)*

After students have completed the exercise, you might want to ask them how this example of unified writing can help them in their own writing.

• Use a controlling simile (my two cultures are like oil and water; they don't mix well).

• Begin and end in a similar way, but do not use the exact same words (begin with the idea that the cultures don't mix and end with the same idea, but use the words *separate* and *distinct* instead.)

Linking Readings

Once you complete Unit 2, you might want to use these questions for discussion: 1. What does each reading contribute to our understanding of how migration affects families? 2. What do the readings in Chapters 5–7 say about how immigrants benefit the host country? 3. What are differences in the migration experience for young people vs. older people, for males vs. females, and for parents vs. children?

Unit Wrap-Up

Word Families *(page 55)*

The following words in the Word Families in Unit 2 show a shift in primary stress. Draw students' attention to them.

discrimiNAtion	disCRIMinate	disCRIMinatory
flexiBILity	FLEXible (-bly)	
MIgrant	miGRAtion	EMigrant
qualifiCAtion	QUALify	QUALified

Collocations *(page 56)*

General Information: Collocations

Collocations are two or more words that native speakers use together. For example:

academic: collocates with *work, problems, achievement*

research: collocates with *findings, report*

put up with: collocates with *a bad situation, a difficult person*

drop out of: collocates with *a program, school, sight*

Learners who begin to notice and use these collocations sound more like native speakers.

There are many types of collocations. For example:

Verb + direct object	commit a crime NOT do/make a crime
Verb + preposition	think + about /of NOT think + in
Various kinds of multiword expressions	back and forth, take care of, adapt to

Learners of a language usually have difficulty recognizing collocations, so it will help if you draw students' attention to them. In the remaining units, you will find a list of collocations for each reading in the Vocabulary Reminder List. If there is no collocations exercise in the Unit Wrap-Up, you will find suggestions in this *Teacher's Manual* for words that collocate broadly. As students increase their sensitivity to collocations, ask them to identify some in the readings. As students begin to notice collocations on their own, suggest that they write them in their word banks.

Short exercises like these using collocations from Units 1 and 2 will encourage students to pay attention to words that are used together.

Match the words on the left with the best choice on the right to form collocations. You will not use all the choices. Use a match only once.

_____ 1. I spend

_____ 2. In difficult times, it is hard to make

_____ 3. There is a growing

_____ 4. You can find

_____ 5. Migrants face

_____ 6. I will learn

a. ends meet.

b. a way to solve most problems if you try.

c. on what she is saying.

d. a lot of time studying.

e. from experience.

f. demand for health care workers.

g. many obstacles.

(Answers: 1. d, 2. a, 3. f, 4. b, 5. g, 6. e)

Fill in the blanks with the most likely collocations.

1. seek _____   (*employment, a better life*)

2. eager to _____   (*please*)

3. depends _____   (*on*)

4. manual _____   (*labor*)

5. left in the _____   (*dark*)

Words with More Than One Meaning (Polysemous Words)

For extra practice, you might want to have students use their dictionaries to find various meanings for these polysemous words in Unit 2: *policy, major* (n., v., adj.), *depressed* (adj.) *concentrate/concentration*.

Recommended Reading

Fleischman, Paul. *Seedfolks.* New York: HarperCollins Children's Books, 2004.

A story about intercultural cooperation and community building among people who get involved in a community garden. An audio version of this book is also available.

Fountas, Angela Jane. *Waking Up American: Coming of Age Biculturally.* Seal Press: Emeryville, (Ed.) 2005.

A collection of non-fiction writings by first generation American women who have experienced the feeling of being between two worlds.

Gallo, Donald R. *First Crossing: Stories about Teen Immigrants.* Candlewick Press: Cambridge, (Ed.) 2004.

A collection of short stories about teen immigrants.

HIGH TECH—PROS AND CONS

Unit Opener (page 58)

As students discuss the questions and quote, you can write words related to the unit topic on the board, either those that the students use correctly in the discussion or those that they need to learn. After the discussion, have students pronounce any new words and check to see that their meaning is clear. Offer definitions and example sentences as needed. Students will probably know most vocabulary needed to discuss the questions, but you might improve the discussion by teaching students words and expressions such as: *access to information, fun, easy contact with family and friends, new ways to be creative (creating games, computer art, etc.), access to age-inappropriate information, online predators, physical inactivity, constant contact with people, being bombarded with ads, scams, etc.*

Ask what the quote suggests about the dangers of technology for children. Many children are so attracted by computers and video games that they no longer play actively outdoors; as suggested by the title of the book from which this quote comes, they are losing contact with the natural world.

CHAPTER 9
Multitasking Madness

Read (page 60)
Recycling Vocabulary

If students used *World of Reading 1*, ask them if they remember the following vocabulary items: *accomplish/accomplishment* (do something that requires effort, something done successfully with effort), *average* (typical, mathematical average), *concentrate* (focus mind on). Call on volunteers to explain the meanings or provide them, if necessary. Tell students they will see these items in the reading, but perhaps with new meanings.

Refer to page 12 for ideas on how to review these words in meaningful activities.

LOCATION IN CHAPTER 9	LOCATION IN EARLIER CHAPTER(S)
actually (About the Reading)	*actually:* "whether the type of friends that adolescents have actually makes a difference" (Chapter 2)
conducting (v.) (¶7)	*conduct:* "who had more conduct (n.) problems" (Chapter 2)
peers (¶11)	*peer:* "Peer Influence on Achievement," "peer pressure" (Chapter 2)

Vocabulary

Vocabulary Building *(page 63)*

Ask students to find two suffixes, one that marks adjectives (*-ive*) and another that marks verbs (*-ize*). Ask them to suggest other adjectives that end with *-ive*, such as: *talkative, active, creative, relative, distinctive, intensive, compulsive, informative, affirmative, primitive, excessive, figurative,* and related to Items 6 and 8, (*competitive*), *addictive.* Do the same for the suffix *-ize: characterize, terrorize, specialize, criticize, unionize, systematize, Americanize, etc.*

Synonyms *(page 64)*

For general comments on working with synonyms, see the comments for the Synonym exercise on page 6.

Item 2, *friends*: *Buddies* and *pals* are informal words; *friends* is neutral.

Item 3, *complex*: *Complicated* is a closer synonym for *complex* since they both include the idea that something has various parts or details; *difficult* is a generic word.

Item 5, *gadgets*: Call students' attention to the word *gizmo* in answer c for item 5. People tend to use this word when they can't remember the name of a mechanical device.

Vocabulary Reminder List

Phrasal verbs: Ask students to find four common phrasal verbs in paragraph 1 of the reading (*sit down, put down, turn on, open up*). These verbs can be used to illustrate the grammar of separable and inseparable phrasal verbs. Two-word transitive phrasal verbs (all of these examples are transitive except *sit down*) are generally separable. You can put a direct object (when it is a noun) either between the two parts or at the end. For example: *Put my cell phone down* OR *Put down my cell phone.* When the direct object is a pronoun, the verb must be separated: *put it down.*

Learners' dictionaries like the *Longman Dictionary of American English* mark transitive verbs [T] and intransitive verbs [I].

log on [I] (¶5) = start using a computer; *take in* [T] (¶8) = think about, put in your mind; *figure out* [T] (¶9) = decide; *take on* [T] (¶9) = accept; *keep from* [T] (¶12) = prevent

Three-word words such as *takes away from* (¶11) = reduces, subtracts from are not separable.

Antonyms: *in touch with* (¶13)/*out of touch with* (¶1)

Verb or adjective + preposition: *concentrate on* (¶8), *focus on* (¶8), *doomed to* (¶13) *Doom* (n.) is another word for *fate* or *destiny*, so *doomed to* means *destined to* with a negative connotation.

Word analysis: *reorient = re-* (back) + *orient* (direct) = direct back

CHAPTER 10

In the Blink of an Eye

Read *(page 66)*

Recycling Vocabulary

If students used *World of Reading 1*, ask them if they remember the following vocabulary items: *available, community, contact* (n., v.), *to found* (an organization), *huge, nonprofit, resident, retire, visually-impaired, volunteer* (n., v.). Call on volunteers to explain the meanings or provide them, if necessary. Tell students they will see these items in the reading, but perhaps with new meanings.

Refer to page 12 for ideas on how to review these words in meaningful activities.

LOCATION IN CHAPTER 10	LOCATION IN EARLIER CHAPTER(S)
give up (¶11)	*gave up:* "I [Powell] gave up the flute, too." (Chapter 1)
achieve (¶4)	*achievement:* "Peer Influences on Achievement" (Chapter 2)
resources (¶4)	*resourcefulness:* "great assets of youth, resilience, resourcefulness, and perseverance" (Chapter 5) *resources:* "pool resources" (Chapter 7)
seek (¶14)	*seeking:* "15 percent of all Mexicans seeking employment in the U.S." (Chapter 5)

Note that the title of this reading is a fairly common multiword expression meaning "very quickly, in a second."

Vocabulary

Vocabulary Building: Synonyms *(page 68)*

For general comments on working with synonyms, see page 6.

Item 3, *autonomy*: The prefix *auto-* (from Greek) means 'self.' Other words with this prefix include: *automobile* (self + mobile/moving), *autograph* (self + write), *autobiography* (self + life + write + noun suffix).

Item 8, *saturate the market*: *Saturate* means "get something completely wet so it won't hold another drop of water." Therefore, when the market for some item is saturated, you can't sell or give away one more of that item. *Saturate* is related to *satisfy*; both come from the Latin word for *enough*.

Vocabulary Reminder List

Phrasal Verbs: *send out* [T] (¶9, 13)

Collocations: *make (something) available to* (subhead), *achieve/gain autonomy* (¶4), *the news spread* (¶6) (also *spread the news*), *all of a sudden* (¶7), *never dreamed it would come to this* (¶9), *defray the costs for/of* (¶10), *put effort and time into* (¶11), *give credit to* (¶12), *a ball of energy* (¶13), *show no signs of slowing down* (¶16), *keep (me) out of mischief* (¶17), *can't wait to get started* (¶18)

Synonyms: *about, roughly* (¶8) = *approximately*

Modifiers of Nouns: The reading in this chapter lends itself well to a review of different structures that modify nouns. Ask students to find examples of the following kinds of modifiers:

Participial Adjectives (*-ing/-ed*): *improving technology* (¶2), *handicapped people* (¶4), *visually-impaired people* (¶4), *donated computers* (¶5, 13) *voice-synthesized software* (¶5), *text-enlarging software* (¶5), *life-changing computers* (¶6)

Compound Adjectives: *voice-synthesized software* (¶5), *text-enlarging software* (¶5)

Noun Modifiers (nouns used as if they were adjectives): *computer technology, voice synthesizer* (¶2), *word processor* (¶2), *turnkey computer system* (¶10), *TPCI and NTPCUG volunteers* (¶12), *Lake Highlands resident* (¶12), *computer service* (¶14), *community event* (¶14), *computer center* (¶15)

Word analysis: *incredible in-* (not) + *cred-* (Latin root to believe) + *-ible* (able, adjective suffix) = *unbelievable*. Knowing the root *cred* = "believe" may help students with several other high-level words: *credible, credibility, creed, credo, credence, incredulous, credulity.*

CHAPTER **11**

Advertisers Try New Ways to Get into Your Head

Read *(page 71)*

Recycling Vocabulary

If students used *World of Reading 1*, ask them if they remember the following vocabulary items: *advertising, ads, founder* (of a business or organization). Call on volunteers to explain the meanings or provide them yourself, if necessary. Tell students they will see these items in the reading, but perhaps with new meanings.

Refer to page 12 for ideas on how to review these words in meaningful activities.

LOCATION IN CHAPTER 11	LOCATION IN EARLIER CHAPTER(S)
analyze (¶6)	*analyses:* "In one set of analyses, we were able to contrast the influence of best friends with the influence of parents." (Chapter 2)
tracking (¶13)	*tracking:* "By tracking students over a three-year period" (Chapter 2)
determine (¶6)	*determined:* "Young people on the move are determined." (Chapter 5)
marketers (¶1), *marketing* (¶7), *supermarket* (¶11)	*market:* "I [Langford] thought two years ago we had saturated the market." (Chapter 10)
ethnicity (¶6)	*ethnic:* "Bosnians leaving behind the ethnic conflicts in the former Yugoslavia" (Chapter 7)

Vocabulary

Vocabulary Review *(page 74)*

After students have completed the exercise, you might want to review words that can function as both nouns and verbs. You can use these words from the reading:

monitor (¶1)   Surveillance cameras monitor our shopping behavior. / I bought a flat screen monitor for my computer.

target (¶8)   They targeted the ad at college students. / Hold the gun steady and aim at the target.

rate (¶11)   The interest rate is low now. / The market researchers asked us to rate the products from best to worst.

Vocabulary Reminder List

Phrasal verbs: *tune out* [T] (¶4) = pay no attention to; *put up* [T] (¶6) = show

Collocations: *raise the/your rates* (¶11)

CHAPTER 12
"21"

Read *(page 76)*

Recycling Vocabulary

If students used *World of Reading 1*, ask them if they remember the following vocabulary items: *overweight, identify.* Call on volunteers to explain the meanings or provide them yourself, if necessary. Tell students they will see these items in the reading, but perhaps with new meanings.

Refer to page 12 for ideas on how to review these words in meaningful activities.

LOCATION IN CHAPTER 12	LOCATION IN EARLIER CHAPTER(S)
ashamed (¶2)	*ashamed:* "felt ashamed that I [Tumang] couldn't relate to my relatives" (Chapter 8)
distinctive (¶3)	*distinct:* "The two identities . . . were separate and distinct." (Chapter 8)

Comprehension Check

Second Reading *(page 77)*

Remind students that if there is no evidence in the text the statement will be an unreasonable inference. Coming to a conclusion with absolutely no evidence is often called "jumping to a conclusion." Jumping to a conclusion is not a good thing to do.

Vocabulary

Vocabulary Building: Synonyms *(page 78)*

Remind students that synonyms will almost always have slight differences in meaning and use. You can illustrate this with some of the words practiced in this section.

Item 2, *ashamed* (feeling shame) has a strong negative meaning; therefore, *embarrassed* is a closer synonym than *uncomfortable*.

Item 4, *triggered* is a verb that comes from a noun. The *trigger* is the part of a gun that you pull with your finger to fire the gun (start the bullet on its trip).

Item 7, *unique* comes from the Latin word for *one* (*uno*). If students know the card game *Uno*, this will be an easy word to remember.

Item 8, *deduce* and *infer* are formal words that refer to coming to a conclusion using clear thinking; *guess* doesn't usually involve systematic thinking unless a person says *make an educated guess*.

Vocabulary Review *(page 78)*

You can use this exercise to review words that function as both nouns and verbs. For example: Put *purchase* (¶2), *trigger* (¶2), and *range* (¶3) on the board. Assign different groups of students to write two sentences for one of the words, one using the word as a noun and the other as a verb. Tell them to consult their dictionaries if the uses in the reading don't provide enough help.

Example answers:

purchase: I didn't make any purchases today. / I didn't purchase anything today.

trigger: The rock star's arrival nearly triggered a riot. / He pulled the trigger on the gun.

range: The cost of this item ranges from $12 to $15. / We found a wide range of prices for this product.

Vocabulary Reminder List

Phrasal verbs: You can use this exercise to review phrasal verbs from this chapter.

Underline the main verb in each sentence and state what the verb means.

1. Mary <u>cut</u> the meat in small pieces. (use a knife)

   I need to <u>cut down on</u> bread. (reduce)

   The forest rangers <u>cut down</u> a few trees. (fell the tree, took the tree out)

2. This room is <u>crying out for</u> change. (urgently calling for / needing)

   Our baby <u>cries</u> a lot. (produces tears)

   The crowd <u>cried out</u> in anger. (screamed, shouted)

3. The child <u>ran away from</u> home. (left, escaped)

   I had to <u>run</u> to catch the bus. (move fast on your feet)

   Our team <u>ran away with</u> the competition. (won easily)

Collocations: *stand in line* (¶1), *swipe a credit card* (¶3), *buy one, get a second (one) free* (¶4); also *buy one, get one free*

Text Analysis *(page 79)*

If students are interested in other differences in the vocabulary of British and American English, have them go to http://www.uta.fi/FAST/US1/REF/usgbdiff.html#a2b. They can also look for similar lists using an Internet search engine.

Linking Readings

Once you complete Unit 3, you might want to use this question for discussion:

Chapters 11 and 12 reveal a negative view of the use of technology by marketers and advertisers. What, if any, are some positive uses of technology in marketing and advertising?

Unit Wrap-Up

Word Families *(page 80)*

The following words in the Word Families in Unit 2 show a shift in primary stress. Draw students' attention to them.

ADdict	adDICtion	adDICtive
anXIety	ANxious	ANxiously
SEquence	seQUENtial(-ly)	

Words with More than One Meaning (Polysemous Words)

For extra practice, you might want to have students use their dictionaries to find various meanings for these polysemous words in this unit: *complex* (adj., n.), *concentrate/concentration, dedication, rate* (n., v.).

Recommended Readings

Bradbury, Ray. "The Pedestrian" *Bradbury Stories: 100 of His Most Celebrated Tales.* New York: Harper Collins, 2003.

This 1950s science fiction story satirizes the effect of television, a new technology in the 1950s, on people's lives.

Asimov, Isaac. "The Fun They Had" *Earth is Room Enough.* New York: Doubleday, 1957. Also in Baker and Blau. *Building on Basics,* White Plains, Pearson Longman, 1999.

This futuristic story is about children who are educated by computer at home.

UNIT 4 LOOKING FOR LOVE

Unit Opener *(page 84)*

As students discuss the questions and quote, you can write words related to the unit topic on the board, either those that the students use correctly in the discussion or those that they need to learn. After the discussion, have students pronounce any new words and check to see that their meaning is clear. Offer definitions and example sentences as needed. Students will probably know most vocabulary needed to discuss the questions, but you might improve the discussion by teaching students words and expressions such as: *chance meetings, shared interests, stability, companionship, excitement, dating.*

CHAPTER 13
Students Think Love Conquers All

Read *(page 85)*

Recycling Vocabulary

If students used *World of Reading 1,* ask them if they remember the following vocabulary items: *average* (typical, mathematical average), *lead to* (cause, result in), *set someone up for* (put someone in a position for/to). Call on volunteers to explain the meanings or, if necessary, provide them yourself. Tell students they will see these items in the reading, but perhaps with new meanings.

Refer to page 12 for ideas on how to review these words in meaningful activities.

LOCATION IN CHAPTER 13	LOCATION IN EARLIER CHAPTER(S)
average (¶5) (typical)	*average* (mathematical average): "Teens also spend an average of six-and-a-half hours a day online!" (Chapter 9)
disappointment (¶7)	*disappoint:* "painful for me [Powell] to disappoint my father" (Chapter 1)
expect (¶1), *expectations* (¶2)	*unexpected:* "an unexpected opportunity for revival" (Chapter 7)
marital (¶2)	*premarital:* "compared to my premarital days when I [Rajini] had absolutely no control over my life" (Chapter 6)
unrealistically (¶6)	*realistic:* "If you have 120 MySpace pals, be realistic with how you communicate with them." (Chapter 9)
tough (¶7)	*tough:* "although the work [nursing] can be tough" (Chapter 6)

Comprehension Check

Second Reading *(page 86)*

You might want to have students write a summary of this research and its findings, using the information elicited in this exercise. This could be done individually, in pairs, or in small groups.

Vocabulary

Vocabulary Reminder List

Collocations: *when it comes to* (¶1) states a topic—similar to *on the subject of / speaking of*; *keep getting better and better* (¶1); *I'll go ahead and (do something)* (¶3) indicates that something you were possibly going to do is now definite; *complete a questionnaire* (¶5) (also *fill out* a *questionnaire*)

Antonyms: *optimistic/pessimistic, satisfaction/dissatisfaction, casual/formal, realistic/unrelalistic*

Read *(page 90)*

Recycling Vocabulary

If students used *World of Reading 1*, ask them if they remember the following vocabulary items: *call for* (a boycott, meaning *ask for*) and *sensitivity* (to cultural differences). Call on volunteers to explain the meanings or provide them yourself, if necessary. Tell students they will see these items in the reading, but perhaps with new meanings.

Refer to page 12 for ideas on how to review these words in meaningful activities.

LOCATION IN CHAPTER 14	LOCATION IN EARLIER CHAPTER(S)
tradition (¶5)	*traditional:* "liberation from traditional restrictions" (Chapter 6)
cute (¶6)	*cute:* "Look at how cute she [Tumang] is, she actually knows all of the words." (Chapter 8)
absolutely (¶6)	*absolutely:* "premarital days when I [Rajini] had absolutely no control over my life" (Chapter 6)
terrible (¶6)	*terrible:* "make up for the terrible loneliness" (Chapter 6)
bothered (¶7)	*bother:* "At first my disability did not bother me." (Chapter 3)

After doing this reading, students could interview an older relative or friend using these questions: *What was dating like when you were young? If dating was not the custom, how did people meet potential partners? Are you married? How did you meet your partner?* Students could then present an oral report to a small group or the entire class.

Vocabulary

Vocabulary Building

Synonyms *(page 92)*

For general information on working with synonyms, see page 6.

Call students' attention to the meanings of the following words:

Item 1, *guys:* When Feynman was growing up, *guys* referred to boys or men. Today, people use it to refer to mixed groups and to females.

Item 2, *sophisticated* comes from a Greek word meaning "to become wise." Today, it includes the meaning of having knowledge of the world. Therefore, *experienced* is a closer synonym than *grown up*.

Item 3, *embarrassing:* In this context, *embarrassing* is perhaps closer to *awkward* (uncomfortable). *Humiliating* (feeling small) may be a bit too strong.

Item 7, *cute* is used for younger people; *attractive* and *good-looking* are used for adults.

Item 11, *sensitive:* In addition to *concerned* or *worried, sensitive* suggests the person is easily made to feel bad.

Multiword Expressions *(page 93)*

Item 5: *call for; I'll call for you at 7:00* sounds dated. Nowadays people usually say *I'll pick you up at 7:00.*

Vocabulary Reminder List

Phrasal verbs: *get in with* (¶1) = join a group; *go out with* (¶1) = go on a date; *get off* (¶5) = leave a bus, train or plane; *take out* (¶13) = go on a date with

In order to understand a writer's meaning, students must recognize the difference between a phrasal verb and a verb plus an adverbial phrase (which answers the question *where?*). This reading gives you four good examples to show students.

PHRASAL VERB	VERB + ADVERBIAL PHRASE
Would you like to **go out** on Sunday? = go out / on Sunday	Go out on a jetty = go / out on a jetty
We're going to **run out of** milk. = run out of / milk (the milk is almost gone)	Run out onto the rocks = run / out onto the rocks
When will you **come back/be back/go back**? (These phrasal verbs with *back* mean "return.")	Pushes her back to the group = pushes her / back to the group
The guys were just **standing around**. (Here *standing around* is a phrasal verb meaning "doing nothing or wasting time.")	Pretty soon, the guys are all standing around me = standing / around me

Verb or Adjective + preposition: *compliment* (someone) *on* (¶6); *worried about* (¶7); *sensitive about* (¶7)

CHAPTER **15**

Googling Your Date

Read *(page 95)*

Recycling Vocabulary

If students used *World of Reading 1*, ask them if they remember the following vocabulary items: *focus* (concentrate attention on), *initial* (first). Call on volunteers to explain the meanings or, if necessary, provide them yourself. Tell students they will see these items in the reading, but perhaps with new meanings.

Refer to page 12 for ideas on how to review these words in meaningful activities.

LOCATION IN CHAPTER 15	LOCATION IN EARLIER CHAPTER(S)
actual (¶19)	*actually:* "Look how cute she is; she actually knows all the words!" (Chapter 8)
amazed (¶15)	*amazing:* "It's amazing how much more time I have." (Chapter 9)
apparent (¶19)	*apparently:* "Apparently, I would not be a jock or a musician." (Chapter 1)
contact (¶18)	*contacted:* "a woman there contacted them seeking help for her grandson." (Chapter 10)
find out (¶9)	*found out:* "I [Angie] finally found out who my real friends were." (Chapter 3)
focus (n.) (¶17)	*focus:* "it [your brain] will focus on taking in the information from the book." (Chapter 9)
initial (¶7)	*initially:* "Initially," she says, "I [Rajini] was very frightened." (Chapter 6)
marketing (¶4)	*market:* "I [Langford] thought two years ago we had saturated the market." (Chapter 10)
networking (¶9)	*networks:* "they lose the networks of family and friends" (Chapter 5)
obsession (¶20)	*obsessive:* "that causes obsessive multitasking" (Chapter 9)
track (¶8)	*tracking:* "By tracking students over a three-year period" (Chapter 2); "retailers are tracking their habits" (Chapter 11)

Vocabulary

Vocabulary Reminder List

Phrasal Verbs: *check out* [T] (¶2, ¶9) = investigate, get information on; *find out* [T] (¶9) = learn; *look up* [T] (¶10) = search for, try to find; *ask out* [T] (¶11) = ask for a date; *dig up / dug up* [T] (¶15) = find / found

Collocations: *largely a matter of* (¶1); *for better or worse* (¶3); *use (something) to your advantage* (¶4); *voice of experience* (¶6); *do online research* (¶6); *not my scene* (¶7); *on-again, off-again* (¶8); *talking points* (¶12); *tell the truth about* (¶16); *there's nothing wrong with* (¶17)

Text Analysis *(page 99)*

After students have completed the exercise, you might want to do another text analysis activity. Put the word *contemporary* and the phrase *tone of writing* on the board. Ask for their definitions and write them on the board. (*Tone of writing* refers to the way it sounds to the reader, for example funny/serious; formal/informal. *Contemporary* means 'current.')

Ask students how the writing in "Googling Your Date" sounds to them, especially when compared to "Untitled" in Chapter 14. Someone might use the word *contemporary*, or perhaps *modern* or *up-to-date*. Discuss with students what they think makes the writing sound contemporary or modern. Examples include the topic (dating using the Internet) and the language used. The phrasal verbs *check something out* and *dig something up* sound contemporary, as do the expressions *not my scene* and *talking points.*

CHAPTER 16
Finding a Wife

Read *(page 100)*

Recycling Vocabulary

If students used *World of Reading 1*, ask them if they remember the following vocabulary items: *foolish, release* (to let go or free energy), *scary/scared*. Call on volunteers to explain the meanings or, if necessary, provide them yourself. Tell students they will see these items in the reading, but perhaps with new meanings.

Refer to page 12 for ideas on how to review these words in meaningful activities.

LOCATION IN CHAPTER 16	LOCATION IN EARLIER CHAPTER(S)
aimlessly (¶13)	*aimless:* "I [Powell] was a happy-go-lucky kid, amenable, amiable, and aimless." (Chapter 1)
casually (¶7)	*casual:* "four different stages of a relationship: casual dating, etc." (Chapter 13)
host (¶5)	*host:* "largely depends on the host countries' policies" (Chapter 5)
long to (¶13)	*longings:* "The joys and longings my parents experienced" (Chapter 8)
sole (¶12)	*solely:* "don't concentrate solely on their homework" (Chapter 9)

If students ask about the word *chuckle*, explain that it refers to a specific kind of laughing—laughing quietly to oneself.

Vocabulary

Vocabulary Reminder List

Phrasal verbs: *turn to* (¶2) = begin again to think about, return to a topic; *give in* (¶4) = agree to something you were originally against; *clean up* (¶7) = clean completely and throw away; *start back* (¶8) = begin to return; *wash down* (¶10) = drink something to help swallow food; *come up to* (¶11) = be as tall as; *drive back* (¶13) = return by car

Verb + preposition: *stare at* (¶9); *snack on* (¶10)

Text Analysis *(page 107)*

Note that, although this selection is autobiographical, the typical pattern of fictional storytelling applies to it.

Linking Readings

Once you complete Unit 4, you might want to use these questions for discussion: 1. What are the similarities and differences between older, traditional ways of dating, as described by Feynman and Soto, and high tech courtship and love? 2. Do people who meet on the Internet have the same expectations and idealism as those described in Chapter 13? Explain.

Unit Wrap-Up

Word Families *(page 108)*

When discussing line 8 in the chart, you can illustrate that which negative prefix is used is arbitrary. Even though people say *satisfaction* and *dissatisfaction*, they say *satisfactory* and *unsatisfactory*, not *dissatisfactory*.

If students are confused about when to use each participial adjective in Rows 1, 3 and 5, put these examples on the board:

amaze/embarrass/fascinate (v.) The story *amazed/embarrassed/fascinated* me.

I was *amazed/embarrassed/fascinated* (by the story).

The story was *amazing/embarrassing/fascinating*.

Ask students to study the examples and answer these questions.

1. Which form (*-ing* or *-ed*) is used to describe the cause of the feeling? (-ing)
2. Which form is used to describe the way people feel? (-ed)

Sensitive (Row 9) is a polysemous word (sensitive person, instrument, skin, topic). You might want to have student use their dictionaries to deepen their understanding of this word.

The following words in the Word Families in Unit 4 show a shift in primary stress. Draw students' attention to them.

curiOSity	CUrious (-ly)		
expecTAtion	exPECT	exPECTant (-ly)	
fasciNAtion	FAScinate	FAScinated	FAScinating
OPtimism	optiMIStic (-ally)		
satisFACtion	SATisfy	SATisfied	satisFACtory
sensiTIVity	SENsitize	SENsitive (-ly)	

Collocations: If you want to deal with words that collocate with several others, there are some examples in this unit: *tough* love/luck/situation; *casual* dating/clothes/remark; *set someone up for* problems/difficulties/trouble/disappointment.

Recommended Readings and Websites

Hagopian, Richard. "Wonderful People" *The Dove Brings Peace*. Farrar & Rinehart, 1944. Also in *Love without Borders*. Pearson, 2001.

In this story a young man tells about his attraction to a rather unglamourous young woman.

Wallis Dolgeville, Claudia. "A Very Special Wedding." *Time Magazine* (July 24, 2006).

This article is about a Down Syndrome couple.

http://drbenkim.com/articles-marriage.html (accessed 02-08-09) "Some Thoughts on Choosing a Life Partner"

This site has an excerpt on choosing a life partner from *Letters to My Son: A Father's Wisdom on Manhood, Life, and Love,* by Kent Nerburn.

Unit Opener *(page 112)*

As students discuss the questions and quote, you can write words related to the unit topic on the board, either those that the students use correctly in the discussion or those that they need to learn. After the discussion, have students pronounce any new words and check to see that their meaning is clear. Offer definitions and example sentences as needed. Students will probably know most vocabulary needed to discuss the questions, but you might improve the discussion by teaching students words and expressions such as: *knowledge, ambition, an innovative idea, willingness to take a risk, provide jobs, earn a living.*

If students know the word *eager/eagerly,* which was a target in Chapter 5, they should be able to infer some meaning for *reluctantly* in the quote *(without much excitement, not wanting to do something very much).*

CHAPTER 17
Entrepreneurs Recognize Opportunities

Read *(page 113)*

Recycling Vocabulary

Refer to page 12 for ideas on how to review these words in meaningful activities.

LOCATION IN CHAPTER 17	LOCATION IN EARLIER CHAPTER(S)
argue (¶6) (explain using logic)	*argue* (disagree): "argue whether we should buy a quart of beer" (Chapter 16)
ashamed (¶19)	*ashamed:* "A large part of me felt ashamed that I [Tumang] couldn't relate to my relatives." (Chapter 8)
competitive, competition (¶14, ¶20)	*competing:* "the competing tasks can't be too complicated" (Chapter 9)
efficiently (¶13)	*efficiently:* "The result is that neither task is done efficiently." (Chapter 9)
initially (¶18)	*initially:* "Initially," she [Rajini] says, "I was very frightened." (Chapter 6) *initial:* "the initial awkwardness of a first date" (Chapter 11)
resources (¶6, ¶13, ¶21)	*resources:* "handicapped people find services and resources" (Chapter 10)
rewarding (¶13), *rewards* n. (¶23)	*rewarding:* "most young people find [moving abroad] a rewarding experience" (Chapter 5)

Since students are reading a selection from a textbook which has clear objectives and which they have previewed, they should read carefully on the first reading, using the glossary on pages 140–141 as needed. Tell them, however, not to expect that they will be able to meet the performance objectives on only one reading. In fact, in a university setting, it is advisable to do the first reading before a lecture and reread the material after it.

Vocabulary

Vocabulary Building *(page 119)*

Items 1 and 5, *innovative* and *renovate*: The root of these two words (*nov-*) comes from the Latin word for *new*. Therefore, *innovative* ideas provide something new, and *renovate* means to "make new again."

Item 3, *undertook* : The word *undertake* is a rather formal word which has the connotation of doing something big and important, or something that will require effort.

Item 8, *ventures*: The noun *venture* is a business term, rarely used outside the field, for example, a business/real estate/farming/speculative venture. Connecting the meaning of business risk to the word *adventure* (also sometimes risky) might help students remember the meaning.

Item 9, *evaluated*: You can help students remember the word *evaluate* "to consider and judge the value of something" if they recognize the word *value* in it.

Item 10, *motivating*: The word *motivating* comes from a Latin word meaning "to move"; a motivating dream moves the entrepreneur to act.

Vocabulary Reminder List

Collocations: *no business experience* (¶2), *as far as (earnings) are concerned* (¶4), *recognize an opportunity and jump on it* (¶5), *impose trade barriers* (Global Impact), *enforce restrictions/rules* (Global Impact), *drive someone out of business* (¶13), *standard of living* (¶17), *make a profit* (¶18), *lay out cash* (¶18), *set up operations* (¶18), *get (a business venture) up and running* (¶19), *that is a signal/sign that . . .* (¶19, ¶21), *financial rewards* (¶23), *own your own business* (¶23)

Verb + preposition: *benefit from* (¶13), *reward someone with* (¶13)

Text Analysis *(page 121)*

As an additional text analysis activity, consider this idea. Readers usually expect a textbook to be informative, objective, and unbiased. Is this true of this selection? Have students discuss.

A good discussion might arise as to whether or not the textbook writer is trying to persuade readers to see the merits of the free-enterprise system. Encourage all opinions that students can support with specific reference to the text.

6565062000

Uploaded to sellyourbooks.com by passedout

¡¡yepoy
Why are your old books are worth
see - anything they have a set and
store. Get the instant price quote
go to sellyourbookbook.com
sellyourbookbook.com¡
¡e sell your books at

CHAPTER 18

I, Lender

Read (page 122)

Recycling Vocabulary

If students used *World of Reading 1*, ask them if they remember t
items: (*challenge* something difficult to do), *dignity, overcome.* C
the meanings or, if necessary, provide them yourself. Tell student
in the reading, but perhaps with new meanings.

   Refer to page 12 for ideas on how to review these words in m

LOCATION IN CHAPTER 18	LOCATION IN ...
innovator (About the Reading)	*innovative:* "innovati ...
manage (Question for ¶7)	*manage:* "some employees build the cars, some sell the cars, and some manage the company" (Chapter 17)
raises (¶2)	*raise* (increase): "use that info to raise your rates" (Chapter 11) *raised* (lifted): "I opened the beer and raised it like a chalice" (Chapter 16) *raise* (find): "Anyone who can raise the capital" (Chapter 17)
seek (¶1)	*seeking:* "Mexicans seeking employment" (Chapter 5); "a woman . . . seeking help for her grandson" (Chapter 10)
transfer (¶5)	*transferred:* "The joys and longings my parents experienced were transferred to me." (Chapter 8)

Vocabulary

Vocabulary Building (page 125)

This exercise includes four verbs (*pioneer, sort, fund,* and *witness*) that are more common as nouns (note that Longman dictionaries put the noun entry first). Ask students if they know a noun meaning for these words and if they can identify a connection between the noun and verb meanings.

   pioneer   In American history, the *pioneers* (n.) left the east coast and traveled across the North American continent, some reaching California, others settling along the way. *Pioneers* (n.) are the first to do something; people *pioneer* (v.) in some activity when they are the first to do it.

   sort   What *sort* (n.) of person are you? Are you the intellectual type? When you put the same *sort* (n.) of thing together, you *sort* (v.) things into categories.

   fund   Our club raised money to start a *fund* to help children with disabilities. When you use the money in a *fund* (n.) to support some activity, you *fund* (v.) the activity.

witness   There were several *witnesses* (n.) who saw the accident. *Witnesses* (n.) are present when something happens and see it; they *witness* (v.) the incident.

Using a Dictionary *(page 125)*

Ask students why they think the entries for *raise* and *shot* on page 126 use capital letters in blue *(to indicate different meanings of a polysemous word)*.

Vocabulary Reminder List

Phrasal verbs: *go along* (¶3) = accompany, *set up* = organize, begin, prepare for use (e.g., set up equipment, a band, a fund, a business)

Collocations: *send the message that* (¶4), *treat (someone) as an equal* (¶4), *at one point* (¶5)

Word analysis: *microlending*: *micro-* (small) + *lending* = lending money in small amounts. Ask students to suggest other words that use *micro-* (*microbiology, microchip, microwave, micro-analysis.*) Note that *microscope* and *microphone* take small things and make them bigger.

interact: *inter-* (between) + *act*. Ask students to suggest other words that use *inter-* (*interface, interlock, intermediate, intermission, international, intervene, interstate, interview*).

Text Analysis *(page 127)*

As an additional activity, have the class plan a set of interview questions for an entrepreneur. Have pairs of students interview the owner of a business and make a written report following the same format as in the chapter.

CHAPTER 19
How to Be Fair

Read *(page 128)*

If students used *World of Reading 1*, ask them if they remember the following vocabulary items: *challenge* (something difficult to do), *community, expert, reason* (think logically), *self-esteem.* Call on volunteers to explain the meanings or provide them, if necessary. Tell students they will see these items in the reading, but perhaps with new meanings.

Refer to page 12 for ideas on how to review these words in meaningful activities.

LOCATION IN CHAPTER 19	LOCATION IN EARLIER CHAPTER(S)
disproportionate (¶4)	*proportionally:* "proportionally the sharpest decline of any major American city" (Chapter 7) *proportions:* "It [Business] consumes growing proportions of our time." (quote, page 112)
enable (¶10)	*enable:* "job that would enable him [Rajini's husband] to earn as much as he presently does" (Chapter 6)
network (¶2)	*network:* "network of friends" (Chapter 5) *networking:* "social networking page" (Chapter 15)
purchase (¶9)	*purchases:* "He arranged his purchases on the checkout belt." (Chapter 12)
resources (¶10)	*resources:* "Debbi Fields took resources—eggs, butter, . . . and turned them into cookies." (Chapter 17)
take for granted (¶14)	*take for granted:* "allowing him [Langford] to do the things most of us take for granted" (Chapter 10)
wage (¶11)	*wages:* "whole families including children pooled wages to buy those homes" (Chapter 7)

Notice that there are two slightly different meanings for *buyers* in this selection. In paragraph 2, *buyers* refers to companies that buy Fair Trade goods. In paragraphs 7, 9, 10, and 13, the word has the meaning given in the glossary—(a person whose job is to choose and buy goods for a store or company.)

Vocabulary

Vocabulary Building *(page 131)*

Item 2, *disproportionate*: It may help students remember the meaning of the word *disproportionate* if they recognize the word *portion* in it and know that *dis-* is a negative prefix.

Item 3, *launched*: It may help students remember the meaning of the word *launch* if they connect it to *launch pad*, where rockets are sent into space.

Item 5, *deals*: Make sure that students realize that *deals* is a noun here, not part of the phrasal verb *deals with*.

Item 6, *sustainable*: Students may be familiar with the word *sustainable* in the context of the environment. *Sustainable* growth or development uses natural resources in a way that means they can continue to be available for a long time.

Vocabulary Reminder List

Phrasal verbs: *come up with* (¶12, 13) = determine

Collocations: *standard equipment* (¶1), *the old-fashioned way* (¶1), *have money/profit left over* (¶3), *ink deals* (¶8), *How exactly does (something) work?* (¶9), *high-quality products* (¶10), *when it comes to* (¶12)

Text Analysis *(page 133)*

Before completing the matching exercise, ask students to identify the topic of this article *(fair trade)* and the author's purpose in writing it *(to explain fair trade, a concept that many people know nothing about).*

Write the paragraph numbers on the board and ask volunteers to read the correct answers (not just give the letter). Write the complete topic on the board in the correct order.

Talk with students about why they think the author put the topics in this order and how each helps her to fulfill her purpose. For example, in paragraphs 1–2, Kroll begins with a specific example of a benefit of fair trade to get her audience interested, especially since she expects that most people will not know much about it.

Analyzing a piece of writing in this way should provide students with a foundation for organizing their own writing.

CHAPTER 20
VIP, A Conversation

Suggestions for working with this poem are in the student book. In addition, you might want to ask students to think about their personal reaction to this question and share their opinions in a class discussion: Who is the more successful person, the businessman or the taxi driver?

Linking Readings

Once you complete Unit 5, you might want to use these questions for discussion: 1. The readings in Chapters 17, 18, and 19 are all primarily informative; the first is a textbook excerpt, and the second and third are magazine articles for the general public. Ask students to comment on differences that they notice in the way information is presented to the reader *(textbook: very organized, logical order, very clear on definitions of terms, longer paragraphs develop topics in greater depth, text features such as two levels of headings and extra information on free trade in a separate box. "I, Lender": uses interview questions and provides information in the edited answers of Flannery. "Fair Trade": uses quotes to report information, shorter paragraphs which is typical of journalistic writing, informal tone created with two examples of questions leading into a new topic).* 2. What, if any, new things have you learned from the readings in this unit on business?

Unit Wrap-Up

Word Families *(page 136)*

The following words in the Word Families in Unit 5 show a shift in primary stress. Draw students' attention to them.

compeTItion	comPETE	comPETitive (-ly)	
distriBUtion	disTRIButor	disTRIBute	
innoVAtion	INnovate	INnovative	
MANagement	MANager	MANage	manaGErial
meCHANic	MECHanism	MECHanize	meCHAnical (-ly)
volunTEER	volunTEERism	VOLuntary	volunTARily

Polysemous Words

For extra practice, you might want to have students use their dictionaries to find various meanings for these polysemous words in Unit 5: *party (n., v.); shift (n.v.), competition, overlook, transparent*

Recommended Websites

http://www.ja.org/

Junior Achievement

> Junior Achievement is an international organization that teaches young people about starting and running a business. Students can learn about it at the website.

Young Entrepreneur

http://www.youngentrepreneur.com/forum/index.php?page=articles

> Students interested in starting a business will find relevant articles at this website.

http://www.fairtrade.org.uk/

The Fair Trade Foundation

This website will allow students to learn more about fair trade and organizations that participate in it.

In addition to Kiva.org, there are other microlending sites students can examine by entering 'microlending' in a search engine.

FINDING YOUR WAY

Unit Opener (page 142)

As students discuss the questions and quote, you can write words related to the unit topic on the board, either those that the students use correctly in the discussion or those that they need to learn. After the discussion, have students pronounce any new words and check to see that their meaning is clear. Offer definitions and example sentences as needed. Students will probably know most vocabulary needed to discuss the questions, but you might improve the discussion by teaching students words and expressions such as: *scientist, analytical ability, research, talent, diagnose, stamina, a good ear, news anchor.*

Ask students what the quotes suggest about the role of work and career in people's lives.

CHAPTER 21
The Foundations of the Theory of Multiple Intelligences

Read (page 144)

Recycling Vocabulary

If students used *World of Reading 1*, ask them if they remember the following vocabulary items: *challenge* (something difficult to do), *expert, foundation* (charitable organization), *impaired* (visually-impaired) *portion* (of food), *reason* (think logically), *self-esteem*. Call on volunteers to explain the meanings or provide them yourself, if necessary. Tell students they will see these items in the reading, but perhaps with new meanings.

Refer to page 12 for ideas on how to review these words in meaningful activities.

LOCATION IN CHAPTER 21	LOCATION IN EARLIER CHAPTER(S)
amazing (¶14)	*amazing:* "It's amazing how much more time I have." (Chapter 9)
complex (¶14)	*complex:* "The human brain is simply not wired to process more than one complex task at a time." (Chapter 9)
determine (¶1)	*determine:* "analyze shoppers' faces to determine if they're male or female" (Chapter 11)
discriminate, discriminating (¶7, ¶8, ¶10) (distinguish)	*discrimination* (treat differently, unfairly): "racism, xenophobia, and discrimination" (Chapter 5)
environment (¶10)	*environmentally:* "crafts . . . that are made using environmentally sensitive methods" (Chapter 19)
expertise (¶6, ¶10)	*experts:* "but advertising experts say" (Chapter 11) *expertise:* "A service is work that provides time, skills, or expertise in exchange for money." (Chapter 17)
lack (n.) (¶14)	*lack* (v.): "Many [young migrants] lack working papers and cross borders as visitors or tourists." (Chapter 5)
motivations (¶8, 9)	*motivating:* "an entrepreneur with a powerful and motivating dream" (Chapter 17)
peer (¶14)	*peer:* "Peer Influences on Achievement" (Chapter 2)
portion (¶13)	*proportions:* "It [Business] consumes growing proportions of our time" (Chapter 17) *disproportionate:* "intermediaries who take a disproportionate share of the revenue" (Chapter 19)
reason (¶4)	*reasons:* "parents have legitimate reason to be concerned about the qualities and values of their children's friends" (Chapter 2) *reasonable:* "The producers are paid prices that enable them to have reasonable resources for their farms and communities." (Chapter 19)
sensitivity (¶5, ¶8, ¶10, ¶14)	*sensitive:* "I [Feynman] was so sensitive about being a sissy." (Chapter 14)
urban (¶10)	*urban:* "immigrants revitalizing a sagging urban neighborhood" (Chapter 7)

Vocabulary

Vocabulary Building *(page 148)*

Item 1, *remedial*: You might help students remember the meaning of *remedial* if they connect it to the word *remedy* which they may have seen on over-the-counter medicines.

Item 10, *motivations*: The word *motivation* is used with reference to ordinary reasons for doing things; the related word *motive* is more often used in the context of criminal activities.

Item 13, *environment*: Students probably have seen this word in reference to the natural world. Here they see it used to refer to whatever situation a person is in.

Using a Dictionary *(page 149)*

You might want to ask students what the headings in small caps under the entry for *element* indicate *(that the word is polysemous and has quite distinct meanings in different fields)*.

Vocabulary Reminder List

Phrasal verb: *set up* (¶12) = *establish, decide*

Collocation: *broaden our understanding* (¶2)

Antonyms: *narrow/broad*

Multiple Intelligence Inventory *(page 152)*

This inventory can be used independent of the self-evaluation suggested in Responding to Reading #2 on page 151, but if your students have not dealt with Responding to Reading, consider having them do #2 before doing the Inventory.

CHAPTER 22
Styles of Thinking and Learning

Read *(page 155)*

Recycling Vocabulary

If students used *World of Reading 1*, ask them if they remember the following vocabulary items: *guide, modify, (communication) style, success*. Call on volunteers to explain the meanings or, if necessary, provide them yourself. Tell students they will see these items in the reading, but perhaps with new meanings.

Refer to page 12 for ideas on how to review these words in meaningful activities.

LOCATION IN CHAPTER 22	LOCATION IN EARLIER CHAPTER(S)
academic (¶2)	*academic:* "By comparing the academic careers of students who began high school with equivalent grades" (Chapter 2)
achievement (¶5)	*achievement:* "Peer Influences on Achievement" (Chapter 2)
behavior (¶5)	*behavior:* "whether their school performance and behavior changed over time" (Chapter 2)
come up with (¶2, ¶6)	*come up with:* "To come up with fair-trade prices for its goods" (Chapter 19)
cues (¶4)	*cues:* "many different kinds of interpersonal cues" (Chapter 21)
deal (¶3)	*dealing:* "The small farmer is often dealing with intermediaries" (Chapter 17) *deals:* "the company has inked deals with 60 stores" (Chapter 19)
dissatisfied (¶7)	*dissatisfaction:* "such optimistic expectations can result in marital dissatisfaction later in life." (Chapter 13)
evaluating (¶8)	*evaluated:* "like any opportunity, it should be evaluated by taking a close look at . . . " (Chapter 17)
lacking (¶5)	*lack:* "Many farmers and artisans lack easy access to tools" (Chapter 19)
model (¶7)	*model:* "Kiva operates on a people-to-people model" (Chapter 18); "is borrowing from a business model used by greeting card companies" (Chapter 21)
primary (¶5)	*primary:* "which primary grade students were at risk for failure" (Chapter 21)
profile (¶1)	*profile:* "adolescents who began the study with the same behavior profile" (Chapter 2) "If your HMO had a record of your nutritional health profile" (Chapter 11)
reward (¶5)	*rewarding:* "most young people find it a rewarding experience" (Chapter 5) *rewards:* "The financial rewards of owning your own business may not happen until you put in years" (Chapter 17)

Vocabulary

Vocabulary Building *(page 157)*

Item 7, *mediocre*: Call students' attention to the word *mediocre*. Ask students if this word reminds them of another word *(medium)* which should help them remember its meaning. Although *mediocre* means neither good nor bad, it tends to have a negative connotation. Nobody wants to be mediocre, yet many people would admit that their skills are neither good nor bad. *Mediocre*, like *medium*, is based on the Latin word for *middle*.

Synonyms *(page 158)*

Here is another opportunity to show students that synonyms have slight differences in meaning, tone, collocation, etc.:

Item 2, *prestigious* has the meanings of both *famous* and *respected*, so neither b nor c alone is a really good synonym; it means "admired as one of the best."

Item 3, *outstanding* means "standing out or better than all others" and is closer to *superior* ("the highest") than to *excellent*.

Item 10, *in charge of* is closer to *responsible for* than *in control of*. When you are in charge of something, you have responsibility for it, but not necessarily complete control of it.

Vocabulary Reminder List

Collocations: *outstanding* (also *mediocre*) *grades* (¶2); *the important thing to remember is* (¶3); *take (their) cues from* (¶4); *fall into a pattern* (¶4)

CHAPTER 23
No Job Is Beneath You

Read *(page 161)*

Recycling Vocabulary

If students used *World of Reading 1*, ask them if they remember the following vocabulary items: *amusing, criticism, fuel, passion, shift* (v. *move*). Call on volunteers to explain the meanings or, if necessary, provide them yourself. Tell students they will see these items in the reading, but perhaps with new meanings.

Refer to page 12 for ideas on how to review these words in meaningful activities.

LOCATION IN CHAPTER 23	LOCATION IN EARLIER CHAPTER(S)
deserving (¶4)	*deserve:* "I [Bibi] want to be paid what I deserve." (Chapter 6)
focused (¶3)	*focus:* "the focus should remain on face-to-face interaction to make a final judgment [about a person]." (Chapter 15)
passion (¶9)	*passion:* "Russell Simmons used his own passion for hip-hop to turn rap artists . . . into international pop stars." (Chapter 17)
shift (¶4, ¶8) *shift* (n.) ¶4, ¶8	*shifts* (v.): "The entrepreneur shifts economic resources out of an area of lower and into an area of higher productivity." (Chapter 17) *shift* (n.): "How long is your shift?" (Chapter 20)
tough (¶4)	*tough:* "The work [nursing] can be tough." (Chapter 6); "Marriage can be tough." (Chapter 13)

Vocabulary

Vocabulary Building *(page 164)*

Items 1 and 4, *naïve* and *dilettante* are words that English borrowed from French.

Item 2, *recover*: In the word *recover*, the prefix *re-* (meaning "back") may help students remember that this word means get back to a normal or previous state.

Idioms *(pages 164–165)*

Idioms vary in transparency. Ask students which idioms they think have the most transparent meanings and what words in these idioms help them understand the meaning.

Vocabulary Reminder List

Collocations: *do anything you want* (¶1); *do odd jobs* (¶1); *I have yet to (recover)* (¶4); *You can't short-circuit the learning process.* (¶10)

Text Analysis *(page 166)*

The reading in this chapter can be used to illustrate the connection between a writer, the audience, and the style used. Ask students to show ways that Shriver has chosen her words for her audience of college students. *(The many multiword expressions, some very idiomatic, give her speech an informal tone. She seems to be trying to reach an audience that would appreciate this informality.)*

Words a writer chooses also reflect the person he or she is. Shriver must have an informal side to her personality to give this speech at a graduation. Other people would have made a more formal speech.

Read *(page 168)*

Recycling Vocabulary

Refer to page 12 for ideas on how to review these words in meaningful activities.

LOCATION IN CHAPTER 24	LOCATION IN EARLIER CHAPTER(S)
apparent (¶1)	*apparently:* "Apparently, I would not be a jock or a musician." (Chapter 1) *apparent:* "The crazy stuff usually becomes apparent on the actual date." (Chapter 15)
eager (¶6)	*eager:* "Young people are often more flexible and eager to learn." (Chapter 5)
embarrassed (¶8)	*embarrassing:* "It was most embarrassing" [having the guys force him to ask Barbara out] (Chapter 14)
qualify (¶7)	*qualified:* "a growing demand for qualified workers" (Chapter 5)
resources (¶1)	*resources:* "TCPI helps handicapped people find services and resources" (Chapter 10); "Entrepreneurs add value to scarce resources. Oil is a resource because it is used as fuel." (Chapter 17)
self-image (¶1)	*images:* "I often see clear visual images when I close my eyes." (Chapter 21, Inventory)

Vocabulary

Vocabulary Reminder List

Collocations: *over the last (couple of) years* (¶1); *a small (or large) percentage of* (¶7)

Text Analysis

Using Exact Words *(page 170)*

After doing this exercise, ask students why Fulghum's use of the children's exact words is effective. *(By providing the children's exact words, Fulghum is following a basic principle of good writing—to show things using details, not to tell about them in generalities. The exact words, rather than general statements such as, "The children were enthusiastic," bring writing to life and make it more interesting to read.)*

Linking Readings

Once you complete Unit 6, you might want to use this question for discussion: Which idea(s) from the readings in this unit do you believe are most important for young people to know in order to find their way in life? Why?

Unit Wrap-Up

Word Families *(page 171)*

The following words in the Word Families in Unit 6 show a shift in primary stress. Draw students' attention to them.

modifiCAtion	MODify	(un) MODified
motiVAtion	MOtivate	(un) MOtivated
LOGic	loGIcian	LOGical (-ly)

Words with More Than One Meaning *(pages 172–173)*

Item 7, *tough*: The word *tough* is used in different contexts with slightly different meanings, but it seems to have a central or core meaning. Ask students what they think it is. *(hard, difficult)*

If you want to deal with words that collocate with several others, there are some examples in this unit:

widespread: criticism/corruption/damage/destruction/suffering/acceptance/recognition/ support

remedial: instruction/class/action

prestigious: college/university/law firm/academic journal

outstanding: career/contribution/grades/job/performance/record

pursue: a career in/an idea/ a passion/a degree in/the study of

tough: love/luck/situation

Recommended Readings and Websites

Vonnegut, Kurt. "Harrison Bergeron". *Welcome to the Monkey House*. New York: The Dial Press, 1998.

This humorous story, set in 2081, satirizes the idea that all people should be equal. People like Harrison who are exceptional in any way wear a 'handicap' to bring them down to the level of those who are not exceptional.

Peace Corps

http://www.peacecorps.gov/

Americorps

http://www.americorps.org/

Peace Corps and Americorps are two volunteer organizations that give U.S. citizens an opportunity to be of service. During their time of service, they may learn about themselves and what they want to do in life.

Student Book
Answer Key

CHAPTER 1
My Early Memories

Previewing, *page 2*

1. not clear
2. sports/athletics
3. music/playing the piano

Read, *page 3*

a, b, b, a, b

Comprehension Check

First Reading, *page 4*

1. the shock he got when he put a hairpin in an electrical outlet (a trauma). He also remembers his grandmother scolding and hugging him.
2. happy
3. nothing

Second Reading, *page 4*

1. c	3. a	5. d
2. f	4. b	6. e

Vocabulary

Vocabulary Building, *page 5*

Part 1

1. d	3. e	5. a
2. b	4. f	6. c

Part 2

7. j	9. i	11. g
8. k	10. l	12. h

Handling Nonessential Vocabulary, *page 6*

1. no; a
2. bad; a
3. It was the way to progress or get ahead in their new country; b
4. She was a good student; a
5. no; b
6. good; a
7. close; b

Vocabulary Review, *page 7*

1. involved a trauma
2. scolded, hugged
3. lacked drive
4. disappoint
5. hilarious, gave up
6. looked out for

Text Analysis, *pages 7–8*

Answers will vary, but they should include the following facts:

¶1 One day when Colin Powell was four years old, his grandmother, was taking care of him. He was playing on the floor, stuck a hairpin into an electrical outlet, and got a shock. His grandmother, who was both angry at him and worried about him, scolded and hugged him at the same time. When his parents came home from work, they reacted in a similar way. What Powell remembers most about that incident is not the shock but that he was important to his family and that they loved him.

¶3 Powell was playing baseball with friends in an empty lot. His father passed by and stopped to watch. Powell, who was not a very good athlete, was not doing well at bat. He felt very bad because he hated to disappoint his father. His father, however, never criticized him; the pressure Powell felt came more from himself than from his father.

CHAPTER 2
Peer Influences on Achievement

Previewing, *pages 9–10*

1. b
2. a

Read, *page 10*

a, b, a, a, b

Comprehension Check

First Reading, *page 11*

1. their friends
2. academic/school performance and delinquency (drug and alcohol use, behavior problems)

Second Reading, *page 11*

A. 1. T; ¶1
2. F; ¶1
3. T; ¶2
4. F; ¶2
5. T; ¶3

B. 1. long-term educational plans
2. whether adolescents attend class, how much time they spend on homework, how hard they try in school, and grades; they also influence drug and alcohol use

Vocabulary

Vocabulary Building, *page 12*

1. e	5. d	9. a
2. g	6. c	10. f
3. j	7. h	
4. i	8. b	

Identifying Essential and Nonessential Vocabulary, *pages 12–13*

2. a. E	b. NE
3. a. E	b. NE
4. a. NE	b. E

Vocabulary Review, *page 13*

1. whether
2. findings, conduct
3. concerned, academically oriented, achievement
4. crowds
5. peers

Text Analysis

Topic and Main Idea, *pages 13–14*

1. b
2. c

Finding the Writer's Definition, *page 14*

1. a student whose friends had higher grades, spent more time on homework, had higher educational aspirations and who were more involved in extracurricular activities
2. students who used more drugs and alcohol and who had more conduct problems
3. whether students attend class, how much time they spend on homework, how hard they try in school, and the grades they bring home

CHAPTER 3
It's OK to Be Different

Previewing, *page 15*

1. She was born with a minor case of cerebral palsy (CP).
2. People were mean to her and treated her differently. She shook a little, and she didn't start walking at the same time as her twin sister.

Read, *pages 15–16*

b, a, b, a

Comprehension Check

First Reading, *page 17*

1. Her disability didn't affect her mental abilities, but it made her shake. She couldn't run well, she had trouble writing, and it affected her speech.
2. Kids she thought were her friends stayed away from her because she was different. People made fun of her and were mean to her.

Second Reading, *pages 17–18*

A.   1. F; ¶2
      2. T; ¶3
      3. F; ¶4
      4. T; ¶5
      5. T; ¶6
      6. F; ¶7

B.   1. a, b, c, d
      2. b, c, d
      3. a, b
      4. a, c, d

C.   1. c
      2. b

Vocabulary

Vocabulary Building Synonyms, *pages 18–19*

1. b, c	4. a, c	7. a, c
2. a, b	5. a, c	8. b, c
3. a, b	6. b, c	9. a, b

Multiword Expressions, *page 19*

1. b	4. a	7. a
2. b	5. c	8. b
3. c	6. c	

Vocabulary Review, *page 20*

1. minor
2. mean
3. stay behind, keep up
4. blamed
5. awkward
6. ignore, weird
7. tease
8. willpower, capable

Text Analysis, *page 20*

¶2. d
¶3. b
¶4. f
¶5. a
¶6. c
¶7. e

Comprehension Check

First Reading, *page 23*

1. 8 years old
2. The parent was teaching the daughter to ride a bicycle.

Second Reading, *page 23*

1. The parent is surprised because the daughter rides off on her own. (lines 5, 8–10)
2. The parent expects the daughter to fall. (lines 11–13)
3. Even though the parent is running, the girl grows smaller as she was pulling ahead. (lines 14–17)
4. The daughter is excited and happy— "screaming with laughter" (lines 19–20)
5. She looks smaller, more breakable, and her hair looks like a handkerchief waving good-bye. (lines 15–17, 21–24).

Text Analysis, *page 24*

1. Vocabulary such as *wobbling, pumping* (sight), *thud, crash* (sound)
2. It compares growing up and leaving parents to learning to ride a bicycle.

Unit Wrap Up

Word Families, *pages 25–26*

1. academy
2. achieve
3. alienate
4. analyze, analytical
5. apparent
6. delinquency
7. disappointed, disappointing
8. humiliating, humiliated
9. influential
10. traumatized

Words with More Than One Meaning, *pages 26–27*

1. a, c, b (1) or a (1), a
2. a (1) or b (1), b, d, c
3. a, c, b, a
4. a, c, b
5. c, a, b

CHAPTER 5

People on the Move: Moving Young

Previewing, *pages 29–30*

1. North America, Europe, Oceania (Graph A)
2. Asia, Latin America and the Caribbean, Africa (Graph A)
3. 191 million, 3% of the world's population (boxed information, p. 30)
4. In 1960 there were 75 million people living outside their country of birth (2.5% of the world's population); this increased to 176 million in 2000, and to 191 million in 2005. (boxed information, p. 30)
5. The article will focus on young people migrating, probably without families.

Read, *pages 30–31*

b, a, a, b

Comprehension Check

First Reading, *page 31*

1. Young people might leave home alone to escape violence, war, poverty, unemployment, crime, or persecution. In general, they leave in search of better opportunities.
2. They tend to go to neighboring countries that are better off or to developed countries.
3. Both host and home countries can benefit though the home country can suffer from brain drain.

Second Reading, *page 31*

1. Young people tend to be determined, resilient, resourceful, persevering, flexible, and eager to learn.
2. Receiving countries (host countries), especially those with aging populations, need young workers both unskilled and skilled. They also need professionals to work in areas where there is demand. Immigrants often take jobs that citizens of the host country do not want to do.
3. Countries of origin lose productive labor and qualified, skilled people (brain drain), but often emigrants send money home (remittances) and sometimes return to their country of origin with new skills.
4. Young emigrants, if they migrate alone, give up family, friends, and sometimes their sense of identity, but they gain employment, learn skills, and acquire knowledge of the world.

Vocabulary

Vocabulary Building, *page 32*

Part 1

1. c	3. b	5. f
2. e	4. a	6. d

Part 2

7. k	9. l	11. j
8. i	10. g	12. h

Using a Dictionary, *page 33–34*

1. 2	4. 4	7. 1
2. 1	5. 1	8. 1
3. 1	6. 1	

Vocabulary Review, *page 34*

1. better-off
2. obstacles, assets, integrate
3. qualified, eager
4. flexible
5. discrimination, rewarding

Text Analysis, *page 35*

¶2–3 c
¶4 d
¶5 a
¶6 e
¶7 b

CHAPTER 6
Bibi and Rajini

Read, *pages 37–39*

Part 1

b, a, a, b, a, b, a

Part 2

a, b, b, b, a, a

Comprehension Check

First Reading, *page 40*

Part 1

1. Bibi finished high school and is in nursing school.
2. She plans to leave Suriname and probably go to Canada to work.
3. She doesn't know anything about Canada except that it's cold. (She has an aunt who is a nurse there.)

Part 2

1. Being a "Gulf wife" has been an empowering experience for Rajini. She has responsibility and respect. She has changed and become more self-confident.
2. The primary benefit is more income, allowing them to build a house, but the primary disadvantage is separation.
3. They hope that they will eventually be able to be together, but they are not very optimistic. It may be their destiny to be separated for a long time.

Second Reading, *page 40*

Part 1

1. Bibi is determined; she's not going to drop out. She's hard-working, dedicated, focused; she doesn't have a boyfriend to distract her.
2. She's not concerned. She thinks the home country has to meet her needs if they want her to stay.

Part 2

1. Another disadvantage is that her husband was not there for their daughter's birth and is not sharing in her growing up. Rajini doesn't want a second child under those circumstances.
2. Unnikrishnan only has a high school education, so he can't get as good a job in India as he has in Saudi Arabia. Also, he can't borrow money to start his own business while they still have to pay off the loan for building their house. The other alternative is to find work in a country where the family could be together.

Vocabulary

Vocabulary Building, *page 41*

Part 1

1. e	3. f	5. d
2. a	4. b	6. c

Part 2

1. d	3. f	5. a
2. c	4. e	6. b

Vocabulary Review, *page 42*

Part 1

1. on the horizon
2. contributing, vicious cycle, tougher
3. ambitious, make ends meet

Part 2

1. empowering, oversee
2. evolve, impressed
3. make up for
4. destiny

Text Analysis, *page 43*

Answers may vary. Possible answers:

Part 1

1. plans to leave Suriname to work abroad / in Canada
2. there is a shortage of health care personnel in Suriname / there's a brain drain from Suriname
3. may/will probably go to Canada

Part 2

4. can't get a job in India that pays as much as the job he has in Saudi Arabia
5. they only see each other every two and a half years / Rajini is lonely / Rajini is running her own life
6. she had to oversee the construction

CHAPTER 7

Bosnia's Loss Is an American City's Gain

Previewing, *page 44*

1. b
2. b

Read, *pages 44–46*

b, a, a, b, b, b, a

Comprehension Check

First Reading, *page 46*

1. The bank got busier; business got better.
2. the arrival of Bosnian immigrants
3. The Bosnians turned the neighborhood around—from an economically depressed neighborhood to a thriving area.

Second Reading, *page 47*

A.

	LATE 1800s–1950	1950–EARLY 1990s	LATER 1990s
1. What immigrant groups if any, came to St. Louis?	Immigrants came from Germany, Ireland, Italy, Eastern Europe. (¶6)	The immigrant flow stopped. (¶6)	Bosnians and other immigrants were settling in St. Louis. (¶2, 4)
2. Describe the economy of the city.	It was an industrial, commercial metropolis like Chicago. (¶6)	The city lost its appeal and went into a decline. (¶7–8)	The city is enjoying revitalization; it's making a comeback—at least in the Bevo neighborhood is. (¶2–4, 9–13)
3. How much did the population of St. Louis grow or shrink?	The population grew to 857,000. (¶7)	The population declined from 857,000 to 350,000. (¶7)	The population grew by about 15,000, the approximate number of Bosnian immigrants that came to the St. Louis area. (¶4).

B.

1. There were job opportunities and cheap housing.
2. The Bosnians have a strong work ethic and are hard-working; very few immigrants in the area are on welfare, and families pool their resources to buy houses.

Vocabulary

Vocabulary Building, *page 48*

Part 1

1. d
2. f
3. b
4. a
5. c
6. e

Part 2

7. i
8. g
9. l
10. h
11. j
12. k

Word Parts, *page 49*

1. people who are new to a place [new + come + er (noun suffix)]
2. not expected, not anticipated, that you didn't think was going to happen, surprising [un- + expect + -ed (participial adjective suffix)]
3. (the process of) coming to life again [re- vit + -al (noun suffix)]
4. bringing back to life, making active again [re- vit + -al (adjective suffix) + -ize (verb suffix)]
5. state of not being employed, not working; the number of people who are not working [un- employ + -ment (verb suffix)]

Vocabulary Review, *pages 49–50*

1. revitalize
2. thriving
3. work ethic
4. newcomers, decent, pooling
5. unemployment, welfare, revival

Text Analysis, *page 50*

1. Yes. He does not give his opinion or interpret the facts. (Typical of journalistic writing)
2. No, most are quite long. (not typical of journalistic writing)
3. Yes. ¶ 1–9, 11–15 are short. (typical of journalistic writing)
4. This article is fairly characteristic of journalistic writing; it has two of the three characteristics.

CHAPTER 8
(Un)American

Previewing, *page 51*

1. no
2. her American peers and her Filipino relatives

Read, *pages 51–52*

b, a, b, a, a, b

Comprehension Check

First Reading, *page 53*

1. Her classmates comment on her weird lunches.
2. Contact with Filipino relatives is through audio tapes.

Second Reading, *page 53*

1. Not completely American: Her lunches at school are different; she doesn't totally relate to Barbie dolls, McDonald's, or TV cartoons.
   Not completely Filipino: She doesn't speak or understand Tagalog; she can only sing Tagalog songs with an American accent and without understanding the lyrics.
   She doesn't understand jokes in Tagalog; she can't relate to her relatives like her parents can, and she feels disconnected.
   All of the ways she doesn't feel completely Filipino are related to language.
2. c
3. a

Vocabulary

Vocabulary Building, *page 53*

1.	h	5.	f	9.	g
2.	d	6.	a	10.	e
3.	j	7.	c		
4.	b	8.	i		

Vocabulary Review, *page 54*

1. outsider, signaled
2. ashamed
3. lyrics
4. resonate
5. distinct

Text Analysis, *page 54*

1. ¶2 shows that she does not fit in perfectly with American kids.
   ¶3–8 show how she feels like an outsider among her Filipino relatives.
2. Paragraph 9 is a summary restating the main idea that she doesn't fully belong to either culture, and her two identities remain "separate and distinct," like oil and water. It relates back to the simile presented in paragraph 1, thus unifying the piece of writing.

Unit Wrap Up

Word Families, *pages 55–56*

1. ambitious
2. discriminatory
3. unemployment, employed
4. flexibility, flexible
5. Immigration, immigrants
6. qualifications, qualified
7. resilient
8. revive

Collocations, *pages 56–57*

1. border/boundary/river/bridge (possibly street)
2. bridge
3. finances
4. herself
5. money, resources, wages
6. a machine, business
7. help/solutions/advice
8. employment/a better life
9. leave, start
10. neighborhood/metropolis
11. direction

UNIT 3 HIGH TECH—PROS AND CONS

CHAPTER 9
Multitasking Madness

Thinking about the Topic,
pages 59–60

1. Around 1995 for both mobile phones and Internet
2. Internet access is poorly distributed. There are only about nineteen countries in which 50% or more of the people have access to the Internet; in 100 countries less than 10%.
3. and 4. Answers will vary.

Previewing, *page 60*

1. *multi* = more than one / *task* = job or work *Multitasking* is trying to do more than one thing at a time.
2. The words *madness* and *trapped* indicate the author has some reservations about multitasking.

Read, *pages 60–62*

a, b, a, b, b, b

Comprehension Check

First Reading, *page 62*

1. They are switching back and forth.
2. Brittany has more time to see friends and go to basketball games.

Second Reading, *pages 62–63*

1. Andy thinks it would be hard to concentrate if he weren't multitasking while doing his homework. He also doesn't want to be out of touch with his friends.

2.

SOURCE	INFORMATION
(¶2) Pew Internet and American Life Project	• 87% of American teens use the Internet (2005). • 50% were online daily.
(¶3) Teenage Research Unlimited	• 19 million American teens IM. • 60% have cell phones.
(¶3–5) Kaiser Study	• 13% use a handheld device with Internet access. • Teens spend an average of 6 1/2 hours per day online. • 26% of time on digital media involves multitasking. • Almost 2/3 of youngsters between 8 and 18 are doing other things while doing homework.
(¶6–8) David E. Meyer	• People are not really doing several things simultaneously; they are switching back and forth and working less efficiently. • Meyer claims it can take four times longer to do an assignment if you are multitasking because humans are not meant to do more than one complex task at a time. The switching back and forth itself uses mental energy.
(¶10–11) Ned Hallowell	Multitasking is stressful; working inefficiently leads to failure and frustration.

3. Four solutions are suggested:
   • Keep the time for cell phone and Internet use separate from the time for studying and homework.
   • Don't even try to keep up with an unrealistic number of "best friends."
   • Don't eat in front of the computer.
   • Turn the computer off sometimes and do something different.

Vocabulary

Vocabulary Building, *page 63*

1. g	4. a	7. d
2. h	5. f	8. b
3. e	6. c	

Synonyms, *page 64*

1. b, c	4. a, b	7. b, c
2. a, c	5. a, c	8. a, c
3. b, c	6. b, c	9. a, c

Vocabulary Review, *pages 64–65*

1. devices, keep in touch
2. complex
3. reorient
4. accomplish, simultaneously
5. efficiently
6. addicts, prioritize

Text Analysis, *page 65*

Answers will vary. Possible answers:

By the Numbers: gives numbers: statistics, facts and figures about young people's multitasking and general use of electronic devices.

Brain Drain: shows how multitasking drains or takes away brainpower. The section explains that the brain cannot multitask. If you try to multitask, you work less efficiently, and it will actually take longer to complete tasks.

Make It Simple: explains that we can't do several complex tasks at once; we can only do simple things simultaneously.

Gaining Control: makes suggestions for controlling the overuse of technology; these will help you get away from multitasking so you will work more efficiently.

These headings are somewhat "catchy" but are still descriptive of what each section contains. The author's use of these headings serves two functions: They attract our attention, and they give us an idea of what is in each section, revealing the organization of the article.

CHAPTER 10
In the Blink of an Eye

Previewing, *page 66*

1. on Halloween night when he was 15, about 60 years ago.
2. Blindness made him rely on others, but he did lead a rather normal life: He finished school, got a PhD, married, had children, had a career.

Read, *pages 66–67*

b, b, a, a, b, a, b

Comprehension Check

First Reading, *page 68*

1. They have enabled him to be more independent.
2. TCPI, a nonprofit organization founded by Langford, helps other blind and visually impaired people enjoy the same autonomy he has gained by using specially equipped computers.

Second Reading, *page 68*

1. F ¶2
2. T ¶4
3. F ¶5, 12
4. F ¶5
5. F ¶14–15
6. T ¶8–9

Vocabulary

Vocabulary Building: Synonyms, *pages 68–69*

1. a, b	5. a, c	9. b, c
2. a, b	6. a, b	10. b, c
3. a, b	7. a, b	11. a, c
4. b, c	8. b, c	12. b, c

Vocabulary Review, *page 69*

1. incredible
2. coordinates, donate
3. refurbish, equip
4. recipient, defray, autonomy

Text Analysis, *page 70*

1. a. personal computer
   b. World Wide Web
   c. frequently asked questions
   d. instant messaging
   e. portable document file
   f. for your information
   g. répondez s'il vous plait (please respond)
   h. American Broadcasting Corporation, British Broadcasting Corporation, Columbia Broadcasting System, Cable News Network, National Broadcasting Corporation

2. *Answers will vary.*

CHAPTER 11
Advertisers Try New Ways to Get into Your Head

Previewing, *page 71*

1. most likely to influence a person; students will later learn that it means find out your preferences to influence you to buy certain things
2. new ways high tech marketers influence consumers

Read, *pages 71–72*

a, a, b, a, b

Comprehension Check

First Reading, *page 72*

1. a
2. c

Second Reading, *page 73*

1. Ads are everywhere: subway turnstiles, garage floors, bathrooms, video games. (¶2)
2. • Plasma screens analyze faces of consumers to select ads appropriate for gender, age, and ethnicity. (¶6)
   • Stores such as supermarkets maintain a record of everything consumers buy to create a profile and aim appropriate ads at them. (¶9–10)
   • Surveillance devices monitor the length of time you hold a product that you pick up to look at. (¶13)
3. These tactics can triple sales (raise them by 300%). (¶7)
4. An HMO might use your "nutritional health profile" to adjust your health insurance rates, raising them if they know that you are at a higher risk for disease because your diet is not healthy. (¶11)
5. The writer thinks these uses of technology are an invasion of privacy. (¶14)

Vocabulary

Vocabulary Building, *page 73*

1. e	4. a	7. d
2. c	5. g	8. b
3. f	6. h	

Vocabulary Review, *page 74*

1. bombarded, tune them out
2. target
3. tactic, gender
4. invasion of privacy, rates

Text Analysis, *page 74–75*

1. The advertisers (could be retailers, sellers)
2. The consumer, ordinary people
3. The weapon is advertisements.
4. The reader wouldn't get the idea that the writer believes there is a war on against consumers. The reading would be duller, weaker, and less effective if the writer did not maintain the military metaphor and use the words on the left.

Read, *pages 76–77*

a, a, b

Comprehension Check

First Reading, *page 77*

1. The man's diet is a mixture: He buys Meals for One, canned food; he also consumes rich things like croissants, patisseries, and chocolate, but he does consume fat-free yogurt, some fresh fruit (bananas, grapes), decaffeinated coffee, and he buys vitamins.
2. He seems to live alone: He buys Meals for One and doesn't seem to buy products for women and children.

Second Reading, *pages 77–78*

A. 1. U He is nervous, anxious, ashamed, staring out the window.
   2. U He buys chicken.
   3. U He buys frozen Meals for One and roasted chicken legs (already cooked). He says he ought to do more cooking for himself.
   4. R He never leaves the neighborhood for more than 7 days at a time.
   5. R He doesn't talk to her, stares out the window.
   6. R He uses vitamins, buys fat-free yogurt, and decaffeinated coffee (but he sometimes buys cigars and beer).
   7. U His purchasing profile indicates that he needs to tidy up and that his apartment is stale and needs air freshener. The computer also recommends lemon whitener bathroom cleaner.
   8. U There's no mention about it in the reading, so no such inference could be made.
B. It tells him what he has not bought in a long time and concludes that he must need basics and things to clean up his apartment. It also tells him that he should do more cooking for himself, and reminds him about retail schemes or special offers. It also tells him that the store is open on Sunday. And it tells him to start all over and "tour" the shelves again.

Vocabulary

Vocabulary Building: Synonyms, *page 78*

1. a, c	5. a, c	9. a, c
2. a, c	6. a, c	10. b, c
3. a, b	7. b, c	11. b, c
4. a, b	8. b, c	

Vocabulary Review, *pages 78–79*

1. purchases
2. range, deduce
3. cut down on
4. trigger
5. unique

Text Analysis, *page 79*

1. d	3. e	5. c
2. a	4. b	

Creating an Effect with Few Words, *page 79*

2, 3

Unit Wrap Up

Word Families, *pages 80–81*

1. accomplishment
2. addictive
3. anxiously
4. efficient
5. invade
6. obsessively, obsession
7. priority
8. recipient, receives
9. sequence
10. simultaneous

Collocations, *pages 81–82*

1. the imagination/the attention
2. a large share of the market
3. birth
4. reduce/lower
5. soldiers/volunteers/forces
6. (new) members/volunteers/staff/workers
7. an allergic reaction
8. a protest/a (consumer) revolt
9. under
10. cameras/monitors/systems

UNIT 4 — LOOKING FOR LOVE

CHAPTER 13
Students Think Love Conquers All

Previewing, *page 85*

1. students' attitudes about relationships and love
2. college students
3. that their relationships would continue to get better over time

Read, *pages 85–86*

b, b, b, a, a

Comprehension Check

First Reading, *page 86*

1. that the honeymoon will never end, that their relationships will continue to get better, that their relationships will be better than those of other couples.
2. No. The researchers say unrealistic optimism can lead to disappointment; it's better to see marriage as tough.

Second Reading, *pages 86–87*

A. 1. Professor Andrew I. Schwebel and his student, Bryce Sullivan
   2. Ohio State University
   3. 238
   4. 18–34 years old
   5. single
   6. Stage 1: casual dating; Stage 2: engagement; Stage 3: after five years of marriage; Stage 4: after 15 years of marriage
   7. average Americans

B. 1. b ¶6
   2. c ¶6
   3. b ¶7

Vocabulary

Vocabulary Building, *pages 87–88*

1. c	4. b	7. a
2. b	5. b	8. c
3. b	6. a	9. a

Vocabulary Review, *page 88*

1. optimistic
2. expectations, average
3. lead to
4. tough, marital satisfaction

Text Analysis, *pages 88–89*

2. the expectations
3. the 238 students
4. the relationships
5. the belief that their relationships would be better than the relationships of other couples

CHAPTER 14

Untitled

Previewing, *page 90*

1. Feynman's date with Barbara
2. They were already going out with girls.

Read, *pages 90–91*

b, b, a, a

Comprehension Check

First Reading, *page 91*

1. embarrassed
2. Yes. He said, "I felt terrific."

Second Reading, *pages 91–92*

A.

1. F; ¶1	5. T; ¶7
2. F; ¶2	6. T; ¶10
3. T; ¶5	7. F; ¶12–14
4. T; ¶6	

B.

THINGS BOYS WERE SUPPOSED TO DO	THINGS GIRLS WERE SUPPOSED TO DO
ask girls out	possibly not be ready when the boy arrives
dress nicely	dress nicely (wear gloves)
call for the girl at her house	say, "thank you for a lovely evening" at the end of the evening
get off the bus first and help the girl down	
walk on the outside (the side near traffic to protect the girl from danger)	
bring her back home after the date	

Vocabulary

Vocabulary Building: Synonyms,
pages 92–93

1. a, b	5. a, b	9. b, c
2. b, c	6. b, c	10. b, c
3. a, b	7. a, b	11. a, c
4. b, c	8. a, b	12. b, c

Multiword Expressions, *page 93*

1. b	3. e	5. a
2. d	4. c	

Vocabulary Review, *page 93*

1. guys, embarrassing
2. go out, advice, supposed to
3. called for
4. cute, sensitive

Text Analysis, *page 94*

1. ¶6 I <u>get</u> all slicked up and go/<u>I'm</u> nervous/She <u>isn't</u> ready/her family <u>has</u> me wait/they<u>'re eating</u>/They <u>say</u> . . .
   ¶9 Barbara <u>says</u>
   ¶11 I <u>say</u>/she <u>says</u>
   ¶13 she<u>'s</u> got (*has got = has*)/I say
   ¶14 She <u>says</u>
2. Feynman uses the narrative present to describe the incident when his friends force him to ask Barbara out and also when he is describing the interaction on the actual dates.

CHAPTER 15

Googling Your Date

Previewing, *page 95*

1. using the Internet
2. the way dates go (particularly first dates)

Read, *pages 95–97*

a, b, a, a, b, a, b, a

Comprehension Check

First Reading, *page 97*

1. They might use the search engine, Google, social networking pages such as Facebook, blog postings, or news stories.
2. Getting information about a date on the Internet can help reduce the initial awkwardness of a first date, but you have to act curious and pretend you don't know anything about the person when you really do.

Second Reading, *page 97*

A.
1. F; ¶1
2. T; ¶4–5
3. T; ¶8
4. F; ¶10
5. T; ¶15
6. F; ¶17
7. F; ¶19–20

B. c

Vocabulary

Vocabulary Building, *page 98*

1. b	5. a	9. f
2. d	6. h	10. e
3. i	7. c	
4. g	8. j	

Vocabulary Review, *pages 98–99*

1. contemporary, turn up
2. disturbing
3. initial, curious
4. contact

Text Analysis, *page 99*

¶1–3	b
¶4–8	c
¶9–11	f
¶12–16	e
¶17–18	d
¶19–20	a

Previewing, *page 100*

1. a
2. c
3. c

Read, *pages 100–103*

a, b, b, b, b, a, a, b, a

Comprehension Check

First Reading, *page 103*

1. She was a neighbor, and he saw her on her porch cracking walnuts when he passed her house. Later they started talking and getting to know each other.
2. It was apparently pretty easy—once he got over his initial nervousness and awkwardness.

Second Reading, *page 103*

1. They lived in a "row of broken apartment buildings." They were "college poor." They had to discuss whether they had enough money to buy beer (he had only $1 at the time). They worked at a car wash. They took food from their mother's refrigerator.
2. He thought of her when Rick said they needed a woman. "Walnuts cracking open like hearts" implies his heart was affected by her. He kept looking out the window to see if he could see her. He went out again in order to pass her house. He thought her plants were lucky to be fed by her. He couldn't concentrate on his homework.
3. She fed him a lot of good food.
4. On their first date they looked around in thrift shops; then he spent his last $5 on Mexican food. He held her hand on the way back to the car. They drove around and went back to sit on her porch where he kissed her for the first time.

Vocabulary

Vocabulary Building, *page 104*

Part 1

1.	e	3.	d	5.	c
2.	f	4.	b	6.	a

Part 2

7.	k	9.	l	11.	j
8.	h	10.	g	12.	i

Handling Nonessential Vocabulary, *pages 104–105*

1. laughed; foolish
2. no; rice, raisins, eggs
3. 15 cents / a dime and five pennies; in an ashtray in the bedroom
4. sunflower seeds; a plate
5. Mensa (their cat)
6. a woman
7. a chair, plants, old newspapers
8. sandwiches, milk, her home-baked bread; walnuts
9. to a thrift shop; lamps, couches (furniture)
10. on the table
11. on her neck

Vocabulary Review, *page 106*

1. longed
2. short of, foolish
3. stared
4. bragged
5. scared
6. courtship, chance

Text Analysis, *page 107*

2.	¶3–4	b
3.	¶5–9	d
4.	¶10–11	e
5.	¶12–13	a
6.	¶14	c

Unit Wrap Up

Word Families, *pages 108–109*

1. amazing, amazement
2. curious
3. embarrass, embarrassed
4. expectation
5. fascinating
6. get married/marry
7. optimism
8. satisfied, satisfactory
9. sensitivity
10. suspiciously

Words with More Than One Meaning, *pages 109–110*

1. c, a, b
2. c, a, b, a
3. b, a, c or b
4. b, a, d, c
5. b, a, d, c
6. b, a, a

UNIT 5 THE ENTERPRISING SPIRIT

CHAPTER 17
Entrepreneurs Recognize Opportunities

Previewing, *page 113*

1. What entrepreneurs do; how free enterprise economies work and how entrepreneurs fit into free enterprise economies; how profit works as a signal to entrepreneurs
2. The material is divided into three parts. The title of each part is a major heading in the textbook. Within parts 2 and 3, there are subheadings.

Read, *pages 114–117*

b, a, a, a, b, b, a, b, a

Comprehension Check

First Reading, *page 118*

Part 1

1. An entrepreneur is a person who starts his or her own business.
2. someone who works for someone else's business

3. The money that employees can earn from a business is limited to their salary and any bonuses or stock options they receive. In contrast, entrepreneurs own the profit from the business; they can pay themselves a salary, reinvest in the business, and make (or lose) an unlimited amount of money.

Part 2

1. an economy in which anyone can start a business, also called capitalism
2. The benefits include the fact that products or services that are needed get produced and are provided through voluntary exchange, which means no one is forced to produce, buy, or sell products or services. Competition regulates quality and keeps prices low. A free enterprise economy discourages the waste of resources.

Part 3

1. Profit is a sign that a business is providing something that is needed, that it is adding value to a resource.
2. Because it may take years before a business makes a profit. Also many businesses close, which is not necessarily bad if the entrepreneur learns from the problems or difficulties of the unsuccessful business. If a profit is an entrepreneur's primary motive, it may not be enough to get him/her through tough times. "A powerful and motivating dream" is a better motivation.

Part 1

1. Mrs. Fields Cookies, Apple Computer, Russell Simmons' music business are examples of adding value to a resource.
2. by working in some form of business as an employee or entrepreneur
3. A product is tangible, while a service is intangible.
4. The word *entrepreneur* comes from 17th century French where it referred to someone who under took a project, but the meaning shifted to mean someone who starts a business.
5. as opportunities in a way that others do not, or others may see the opportunity at the wrong time
6. The ordinary use of the word *scarce* means "in short supply," that there isn't enough of something. The term *scarce resources* as used in business means the resource costs money.

Part 2

1. the money used to start a business
2. A small business has fewer than 100 employees and yearly sales less than $5 million; a big business has over 100 employees and annual sales of more than $5 million. Small businesses are more common than big businesses, and most big businesses started out small.
3. Competition keeps prices down while maintaining quality, which benefits consumers. Competition puts inefficient enterprises out of business.
4. This is a metaphor; like the engine of a car, entrepreneurship provides the force that drives the economy. It creates wealth and jobs so people consume more, and living standards improve.

Part 3

1. Profit is the positive difference between the amount of money coming in and the amount of money going out to pay expenses. It is a sign that value has been added to a scarce resource and that something is being produced that people are willing to pay for.
2. If a business fails, an entrepreneur should not be ashamed. He/she should learn from the experience. It may be that there was no demand for the product or service the business was providing, and the entrepreneur should undertake a different business.

Global Impact—Free Trade

1. a tax on imports designed to protect domestic products by making imported products more expensive (Remind students that they have access to the glossary if they need it.)
2. Barriers to international trade have been, to a large extent, removed. Free trade zones like the North American Free Trade Agreement (NAFTA) and the General Agreement on Tariffs and Trade (GATT) eliminate tariffs. (117 countries belong to GATT.) Also shipping is easier than it used to be, and international communication is facilitated by the Internet.
3. No. In ¶ 11 *free trade* refers to free enterprise, an economy based on voluntary exchange. In contrast, *free trade* on an international level means removal of trade barriers, i.e. tariffs, between countries.

Vocabulary

Vocabulary Building, *page 119*

Part 1

1. f	3. d	5. a
2. c	4. b	6. e

Part 2

7. l	9. j	11. g
8. i	10. h	12. k

Vocabulary Review, *page 120*

1. venture
2. regulations
3. resources
4. innovative, evaluate
5. competition
6. eventually

Text Analysis, *page 121*

1. ¶3: the buying and selling of products or services in order to make money
2. ¶3: something that exists in nature or is made by human beings
3. ¶3: can be touched
4. ¶3: work that provides time, skills, or expertise in exchange for money
5. ¶3: can't be touched
6. ¶3: someone who earns a living by working for someone else's business
7. ¶6: someone who starts a new business
8. ¶6: all resources that cost money

9. ¶8: the system by which a country's money and goods are produced and used
10. ¶8: the study of the way in which money and goods are produced and used
11. ¶9: a system in which anyone is free to start a business
12. ¶10: an economic system in which people are free to start a business by raising capital
13. ¶10: money or property used to start and operate a business
14. a trade between two parties who agree to trade money for a product or service
15. ¶18: the difference between the amount of money coming in and the amount required to pay the bills

CHAPTER 18
I, Lender

Previewing, *page 122*

1. Matt Flannery is the interviewee who founded Kiva.org; Amy Crawford is the interviewer.
2. The headings are questions the interviewer asked.
3. The paragraphs under the headings are Flannery's answers.
4. Kiva.org allows private individuals to make microloans to individuals who want to start a small business in developing countries.

Read, *pages 122–123*

a, a, b

Comprehension Check

First Reading, *page 124*

1. from individual lenders in developed countries who choose the business they want to lend to from Internet postings placed by microfinance institutions in developing countries
2. Flannery believes that getting a loan is more dignified than accepting a donation. A loan is meant to help a business get started. It's not a handout.

Second Reading, *page 124*

1. T; ¶2		6. F; ¶5
2. F; ¶2, 3		7. T; ¶6
3. F; ¶1, 3		8. T; ¶6
4. F; ¶5		9. T; ¶7
5. T; ¶2, 5		10. T; ¶8

Vocabulary

Vocabulary Building, *page 125*

1. c	4. e	7. b
2. h	5. a	8. f
3. d	6. g	

Using a Dictionary, *pages 125–126*

1. 1	3. 1	5. 3
2. 5	4. 4	

Vocabulary Review, *page 127*

1. raise
2. microloans, dignified
3. sort, post
4. transparent, witness
5. shot
6. pioneered

Text Analysis, *page 127*

1. Questions are in boldface, followed by answers.
2. There are short chunks of text to handle; each response is directly related to the preceding question.
3. *Answers will vary.*

CHAPTER 19
How to Be Fair

Previewing, *page 128*

1. coffee, clothing, gifts (handicrafts); they can be bought at the donut shop, online, through catalogs
2. The author's purpose is to explain how fair trade works.

Read, *pages 128–130*

b, a, b, b, a, b, a

Comprehension Check

First Reading, *page 130*

1. The underlying principle is the elimination of intermediaries or middlemen so that the original producer gets more of the retail price. In order to do this, the producers have to do things middlemen typically do. This is usually achieved by forming a cooperative among farmers or artisans.
2. The principal beneficiary is the original producer, the artisan or the farmer, who can now earn a living wage because less money goes to the intermediaries.

Second Reading, *pages 130–131*

A.
1. F; ¶1–2
2. T; ¶4, 9
3. F; ¶5
4. T; ¶ 6–7
5. F; ¶ 6, 8
6. T; ¶9–10, 1–2
7. T; ¶10
8. F; ¶11
9. T; ¶12–13

B.
1. Ten Thousand Villages is committed to continuous purchasing and paying for producers in advance. ¶13
2. Some of the challenges are lack of tools (e.g. computers, phones), poor transportation, and political instability. ¶14
3. More than a million family farms in developing countries are now earning more; fair trade farmers that supply Dunkin Brands have earned an additional 3.1 million dollars. ¶15

Vocabulary

Vocabulary Building, *page 131*

1. d	4. h	7. f
2. g	5. a	8. c
3. e	6. b	

Multiword Expressions, *page 132*

1. left over
2. rang up
3. a living wage
4. coming up with, come up with
5. take for granted

Vocabulary Review, *page 132*

1. straightforward
2. enable
3. disproportionate, left over
4. sustainable, living wage
5. certified

Text Analysis, *page 133*

1. g	4. e	7. f
2. a	5. b	
3. d	6. c	

CHAPTER 20

VIP, a Conversation

Comprehension Check

First Reading, *page 135*

1. in a taxi (stanza 1, line 4—"step on it;" stanza 6, line 1—"You're my last fare")
2. the taxi driver and the passenger, who is a real estate developer (the supposed VIP)

Second Reading, *page 135*

Level of agreement (agree/neutral/disagree) will vary, but evidence that should be considered is pointed out.

1. The passenger develops malls, is going to an important meeting, and is in a hurry.
2. The driver works on a shift, makes just enough to get along.
3. The driver sees the passenger as a successful person; in contrast, he sees himself as a humble person (two pieces of evidence: his home is small and he makes just enough money).
4. The driver speaks respectfully; the passenger says *please*.
5. The passenger attempts some modesty (stanza 5), but in stanza 3, he sounds like a big shot. The taxi driver is matter-of-fact about his work and shows no particular pride.
6. no evidence, therefore, response will probably be neutral
7. Stanza 8 sounds positive, but stanza 9 qualifies the comment.

Text Analysis, *page 136*

1. The taxi driver's words are in italics; the passenger's words are in regular font.
2. possibly because the two parts show different things about the taxi driver. The things the taxi driver says in stanza 8 are positive and indicate contentment while those in stanza 9 show his humbleness and self-deprecation implying that he doesn't believe that he is successful. However, if stanza 8 is read to show that the driver is truly content, stanza 9 might sound a bit ironic, indicating that the taxi driver isn't really impressed by the VIP.

Unit Wrap Up

Word Families, *pages 136–137*

1. competitive
2. distribute
3. donate
4. establishment
5. funding
6. invest, investment
7. innovative/innovators, innovations
8. manager, management, managerial, or management
9. mechanize, mechanical
10. voluntarily, volunteers

Collocations, *page 138*

1. company/hospital/program (possibly grants)
2. loans
3. living
4. money/living
5. respect
6. effort/energy/time
7. capital/funds/money
8. prices
9. children
10. Collaborative/Co-operative/Joint

Writing, *page 139*

3. *Answers will vary. Possible answers:*
   a. A product is something tangible that exists in nature or is made (produced) by people. A service is something intangible (time, expertise) given in exchange for money.
   b. Adding value to resources means transforming them to a higher level—coal that heats your house or powers factories; wood that becomes furniture, buildings or paper; flour, sugar, eggs and butter that become cookies. Singers and musicians can be considered resources, and value is added when they produce songs that entertain people who are willing to pay for CDs or some other media through which they can enjoy the performance.
   c. A small business has fewer than 100 employees and makes less than $5 million a year. A large business has more than 100 employees and makes at least $5 million a year. Small businesses are more common, yet even big businesses usually start small.
   d. If all companies were monopolies (the only ones that provided a product or service), they could charge high prices and provide low quality products or services. If, however, other companies provide the same products or services, company A can't charge a much higher price than company B (quality being equal) and expect to sell anything. Likewise, if company A cuts corners to keep prices low, quality will be poor and customers will deal with company B to get better quality. So the free market system, which is competitive, benefits consumers by keeping both prices and quality in check.
   e. Profit is the positive difference between the amount of money that comes in (gross income) and the amount needed to cover all expenses. It is a sign that there is a demand for the goods or services the company provides. If a company does not eventually earn a profit, the entrepreneur is probably in the wrong business and should make a change.
   f. Kiva.org is like a matchmaker. Individuals who want to help entrepreneurs in the developing world can find them at Kiva.org, and individuals in the developing world who need to raise money for their small business (i.e. they need a microloan) can find financing at Kiva. Microlending works well because the borrowers are motivated to repay loans so they can get additional loans in the future. Lenders don't have to put up a lot of money to do a lot of good.

g. Fair trade helps farmers and artisans in the developing world by eliminating middlemen. This leaves a large portion of the retail price in the hands of the original producers, who can then reinvest in the business and still earn a living wage. Farmers and artisans often form cooperatives to do some of the work formerly done by intermediaries. Co-op members pool resources and can invest in such things as farm machinery that they otherwise could not afford.

CHAPTER 21
The Foundations of the Theory of Multiple Intelligences

Previewing, *page 143*

1. a. The Theoretical Basis for MI Theory
   b. The Eight Intelligences Described
2. *Answers will vary.*

Read, *pages 144–146*

a, a, a, a, b, a, b, a, b

Comprehension Check

First Reading, *page 146*

1. b
2. 1. e
   2. c
   3. g
   4. h
   5. f
   6. a
   7. d
   8. b

Second Reading, *page 147*

1. F; ¶2   6. T; ¶8
2. F; ¶3   7. F; ¶9
3. F; ¶4, 8   8. T; ¶10
4. T; ¶5, 6   9. T; ¶13
5. F; ¶7   10. T; ¶14

Vocabulary

Vocabulary Building, *page 148*

Part 1

1. f   4. b   7. d
2. c   5. g
3. e   6. a

Part 2

8. k   11. h   14. l
9. m   12. j
10. n   13. i

Using a Dictionary, *pages 149–150*

1. 2   3. 2   5. 1
2. 1   4. 1   6. 2

Vocabulary Review, *pages 150–151*

1. theory
2. logical
3. reason
4. perceive
5. transform
6. motivations, cues
7. accurate
8. impairs

Text Analysis, *page 151*

1. They are examples of types of work: occupations/professions. Each one requires the indicated intelligence.
2. Parentheses

CHAPTER 22
Styles of Thinking and Learning

Previewing, *page 154*

1. No. Style is how we use the abilities we have.
2. a, b, d
3. b

Read, *pages 155–156*

b, b, a, a, b, a, b

Comprehension Check

First Reading, *page 156*

1. Alex is a successful contracts lawyer. He is good at following other people's instructions.
2. Bill is a successful research scientist. He is good at coming up with his own ideas (thinking for himself).
3. Curt is a successful psychotherapist. He is good at evaluating people and things.

Second Reading, *page 157*

1. e	4. a	7. b
2. c	5. d	
3. f	6. g	

Vocabulary

Vocabulary Building, *page 157*

1. f	4. c	7. e
2. g	5. h	8. d
3. b	6. a	

Synonyms, *page 158*

1. a, b	5. a, b	9. a, c
2. b, c	6. b, c	10. a, b
3. a, b	7. a, c	
4. a, c	8. b, c	

Vocabulary Review, *page 159*

1. styles	5. come up with
2. model, at a loss	6. evaluate
3. contracts	7. compatible
4. came into his own	

Text Analysis, *page 159*

Answers will vary. Possible answers:

1. The definition of *style* in ¶ 1 does not make the meaning come alive; it's dry and impersonal. It gives you no idea about how styles affect the whole person.
2. The author gives details about the academic, professional, and personal (especially related to marriage) lives of the three men.
3. The details are intended to give you a portrait of each individual and to show how each differs from the others even though all are considered highly intelligent.

CHAPTER 23
No Job Is Beneath You

Previewing, *page 161*

1. Shriver's message can be expressed in a number of ways, among them: No one is too good for any job, you should be ready for any job, and don't expect to start at the top.
2. Some college graduates think they are smarter than they really are; all college students have a lot to learn, which they can do only if they accept that they don't know everything. Probably the best way to show that you don't know everything is to be willing to start at the bottom. Also, starting at the bottom builds character.

Read, *pages 161–162*

b, a, a, a, b, b, b, a, a

Comprehension Check

First Reading, *page 163*

1. Shriver's first job was in a training program at KYW-TV in Philadelphia.
2. Her boss was not welcoming and told her in no uncertain terms that he only wanted serious people, not rich, spoiled brats like her who were amusing themselves until they got married. She ran to the bathroom and cried, called her parents, and then set out to prove him wrong by doing every job imaginable in the newsroom.

Second Reading, *page 163*

1. Starting at the bottom builds character and makes you determined to move up. It teaches you that you are not as smart as you might think. It's the best way to learn.
2. The news director didn't want rich, spoiled brat dilettantes who weren't serious. He didn't want anyone who wasn't willing to work twenty-four hours a day, eight days a week.
3. Shriver was willing to work all shifts (including weekends and holidays), search wire services for stories for reporters to do, keep records of reporters' videotapes, listen to police scanners, answer the phone, make coffee for her boss and smile about it; she was willing to do things no one else wanted to do.

Vocabulary

Vocabulary Building, *page 164*

1. g	5. h	9. b
2. i	6. a	10. f
3. j	7. c	
4. e	8. d	

Idioms, *pages 162–165*

1. d	5. j	9. c
2. h	6. f	10. e
3. i	7. k	11. g
4. a	8. b	

Vocabulary Review, *page 165*

1. passion
2. pulled strings
3. spoiled brats
4. naïve
5. bruised her ego, criticism, take the heat
6. pursued

Text Analysis, *page 166*

1. clue you in
2. headed off
3. set out
4. setting up shoots
5. play around
6. fueling
7. brush off
8. dished out

CHAPTER 24
Untitled

Previewing, *page 167*

1. b
2. a
3. b

Read, *page 168*

a, b, a, a

Comprehension Check

First Reading, *page 168*

1. The kindergarten children have more enthusiasm and a more positive self-image than the college students; the college students seem to have lost self-confidence.
2. What happened to the self-confidence and enthusiasm of the kindergartners? What happened between kindergarten and college?

Second Reading, *page 169*

1.
   Anything!   K
   not majoring in the subject   C
   confident in spirit   K
   eager to learn   K
   embarrassed   C
   have not done any of these things since about third grade   C
   No problem!   K
   Of course!   K
   qualify responses with their limitations   C
   Sure, why not?   K
   they do not have talent   C
   Yes!   K

2. b

Vocabulary

Vocabulary Building, *page 169*

1. d	4. a	7. e
2. h	5. g	8. b
3. f	6. c	

Vocabulary Review, *page 170*

1. access, facilities
2. apparent, self-image
3. embarrassed
4. make up
5. qualify
6. confident

Unit Wrap Up

Word Families, *pages 171–172*

1. accuracy
2. critical, criticize
3. intend, unintentional
4. modifications
5. motivate, motivated
6. logically
7. passionate
8. perceptive
9. prestige
10. pursuit

Text Analysis, *pages 170-171*

FULGHUM'S QUESTIONS	CHILDREN'S ANSWERS
¶3 How many of you can sing? What if you don't know the words?	Of course we sing. Anything. Let's sing! Why not? No problem, we make them up.
¶4 How many of you dance? What kind of music do you like to dance to?	(All hands go up.) Any kind! Let's dance. Sure, why not?
¶5 Do you like to act in plays? Do you play musical instruments? Do you write poetry? Can you read and write and count?	Yes! (to all questions) We're learning that stuff now.

1. Yes, of course, no problem! Sure. Why not?
2. Any kind, anything. No problem. We're learning that stuff now.
3. We make them up. (The children also write poetry.)

Words with More Than One Meaning, *pages 172–173*

1. a, d, b, c, f, e
2. b, a,
3. b, a, b
4. c, a, d, b
5. c, c, b, d, a
6. b, a, a
7. c, e, d, b, a

Unit Tests

Test Rationale

Although tests are required as a means of evaluation by educational institutions, their primary purpose should be to solidify learning. Since language learning is a long-term endeavor, tests should be viewed as another opportunity for students to improve reading ability and knowledge of vocabulary.

The tests in this series, therefore, have two goals. First, they provide feedback to both students and teachers on how well students have understood and begun to learn the material of a unit. Second, they give students an opportunity to apply their developing reading abilities to new material.

A corollary of this testing philosophy is that only teachers who are in regular contact with the developing skills of their students are capable of judging the fairness of any test. Thus, teachers should alter tests as they see fit for their particular students or teaching situations.

Test Format

PART 1: REVIEWING (Unit Content)

Paragraph Completion

These exercises, which are similar to the Vocabulary Review in each unit, check students' knowledge of vocabulary items that are central to the content of the unit. Completing cloze exercises correctly depends on knowing both the meaning of the vocabulary items and how they express the central ideas of the readings.

Word Families

These exercises are similar to the word family exercises in the Unit Wrap-Up. They require students to select the correct grammatical form of a word for a new context. They call attention to the suffixes that are commonly associated with the categories of nouns, verbs, adjectives and adverbs, and contribute to developing accuracy in both speaking and writing.

Matching

The matching sections emphasize that knowing a word is more than knowing its meanings; it is also a matter of knowing how native speakers combine words to form multiword expressions and common combinations of words, i.e. collocations.

© 2009 by Pearson Education, Inc. Duplication for classroom use is permitted.

Writing

These questions check students' developing abilities to learn from what they read, an important academic skill. They also help students develop as writers and test takers by offering regular opportunities to write short answers to questions about the readings they have done. Students should gradually get better at writing clear, focused answers. Teachers should decide whether they want to evaluate only the content of answers or both the content and grammatical accuracy of the writing.

There are several ways to prepare students to do well on this section. In the beginning, the questions may be given to students ahead of time to discuss in small groups. Teachers can also add a couple of other questions so that students don't know the exact choice they will have on the test. Over a period of time, advanced knowledge of the questions could be eliminated so students experience the reality of test taking as it is in many college courses.

Part 2: EXPLORING (New Reading)

The goal of *World of Reading* is to enable students to read authentic texts written for native English speakers. Therefore, new readings similar in level to those in the Student Book are part of each test, giving students an opportunity to read additional authentic material, not with the idea of preparing it for class, but with the idea of obtaining as much information from it as possible.

Vocabulary

Although the vocabulary items all look alike, there are two kinds of items: 1) those where the meaning of the word is inferable from context (similar to the marginal multiple choice items in the Student Book) and 2) those where there really isn't enough context. In the latter case, items are designed to encourage students to check that a meaning makes sense. To accomplish this, there are two obviously incorrect distracters; if students are paying attention, this provides the meaning of the target word or expression, as only one choice makes sense. This is preferable to giving students the definitions as glosses because it encourages intelligent thinking and closer attention to the text. A few items, however, are glossed.

Comprehension

Finally, students demonstrate how much of the new selection they are able to understand. In most cases, this is done through true/false items. When you go over the test with students, encourage them to identify the evidence that helped them answer each question. Be sure they understand why the false statements are false.

In the case of some readings, the content does not lend itself to ten good true/false items, so students answer *WH*-questions to demonstrate their understanding.

© 2009 by Pearson Education, Inc. Duplication for classroom use is permitted.

UNIT 1 GROWING UP

PART ONE
REVIEWING

1.1 Paragraph Completion *(10 points)*

Complete the paragraph with items from the list. Use each item only once.

adolescence	bother	concerned about	find out	look out for
alienated	capable of	contented	influence	teased

The readings in this unit point out several factors that have considerable
(1) _____ on growing up. As the Powell reading shows, one of the most
important things in early childhood is the sense of security which comes from having parents
who are (2) _____ their children and involved in their lives. Children also
need to learn to handle difficulties. Although Angie's classmates (3) _____
her because she was different, she learned not to let it (4) _____ her. Another
important factor is that, especially in (5) _____, teenagers need the right kind
of friends; it is not good for them to feel (6) _____ and alone. Good friends
(7) _____ each other and help each other resist peer pressure to do bad
things. As you grow up, you (8) _____ who you are and what you are
(9) _____ doing well. There will be problems along the way, but if you learn
to handle them, you have a better chance of growing up to be a(n) (10) _____
adult.

1.2 Word Families *(5 points)*

Choose the correct form of the word to complete each sentence.

1. Angie's _____ work must have been good; she is now a college
graduate.

   a. academy   b. academic   c. academically

2. In order to be a computer programmer, you have to be able to think _____.

   a. analysis   b. analyze   c. analytically

3. When you go for a job interview, you should have a neat, clean _____.

   a. appearance   b. appear   c. apparent

4. Most children want to please their parents; they don't want to be a
_____ to them.

   a. disappointment   b. disappoint   c. disappointing

5. It can be _____ to be corrected in front of your peers.

   a. humiliation   b. humiliate   c. humiliating

© 2009 by Pearson Education, Inc. Duplication for classroom use is permitted.

1.3 Matching (*6 points*)

Match the beginning of the sentence on the left with the correct ending on the right. Use each match only once.

_____ 1. Angie learned to stick up   a. with her classmates.

_____ 2. Stay away   b. hilarious.

_____ 3. Angie could keep up   c. for herself.

_____ 4. Angie wasn't happy when   d. of people who are different.
she got held   e. from friends who are a bad influence.

_____ 5. Don't blame   f. yourself for your problems.

_____ 6. It's mean to make fun   g. back in fourth grade.

1.4 Writing (*9 points*)

Answer three of the questions. Write two to three complete sentences for each answer, using information from the readings in the unit.

1. What did you learn about Powell's relationship with his father?
2. According to research, how do peers and parents influence adolescents?
3. What does Angie think parents should teach their children about relating to disabled people?
4. What does the poem "To a Daughter Leaving Home" say to parents about how to help their children grow up?

PART TWO

EXPLORING

2.1 Reading

Read the text.

Dealing with Peer Pressure

Defining Peer Pressure

1   Peers influence your life, even if you don't realize it, just by spending time with you. You learn from them, and they learn from you. It's only human nature to listen to and learn from other people in your age group.

2   Peers can have a positive influence on each other. Maybe another student in your science class taught you an easy way to remember the planets in the solar system, or someone on the soccer team taught you a cool trick with the ball. You might admire a friend who is always a good sport and try to be more like him or her. Maybe you got others excited about your new favorite book, and now everyone's reading it. These are examples of how peers positively influence each other every day.

3   Sometimes peers influence each other in negative ways. For example, a few kids in school might try to get you to cut class with them, your soccer friend might try to <u>convince</u> you to be mean to another player and never pass her the ball, or a kid in the neighborhood might want you to <u>shoplift</u> with him.

© 2009 by Pearson Education, Inc. Duplication for classroom use is permitted.

Why Do People Give in to Peer Pressure?

4   Some kids give in to peer pressure because they want to be liked, because they want to fit in, or because they worry that other kids may make fun of them if they don't <u>go along with</u> the group. Others may go along because they are <u>curious</u> to try something new that others are doing. The idea that "everyone's doing it" may influence some kids to leave their better judgment, or their common sense, behind.

How to Walk Away from Peer Pressure

5   It is <u>tough</u> to be the only one who says "no" to peer pressure, but you can do it. Paying attention to your own feelings and beliefs about what is right and wrong can help you know the right thing to do. Inner strength and self-confidence can help you <u>stand firm</u>, walk away, and <u>resist</u> doing something when you know better.

6   It can really help to have at least one other peer, or friend, who is willing to say "no," too. This takes a lot of the power out of peer pressure and makes it much easier to resist. It's great to have friends with values similar to yours who will <u>back you up</u> when you don't want to do something.

7   You've probably had a parent or teacher advise you to "choose your friends wisely." Peer pressure is a big reason why they say this. If you choose friends who don't use drugs, cut class, smoke cigarettes, or lie to their parents, then you probably won't do these things either, even if other kids do. Try to help a friend who's having trouble resisting peer pressure. It can be powerful for one kid to join another by simply saying, "I'm with you—let's go."

8   Even if you're faced with peer pressure while you're alone, there are still things you can do. You can simply stay away from peers who pressure you to do stuff you know is wrong. You can tell them "no" and walk away. Better yet, find other friends and classmates to pal around with.[1]

9   If you continue to face peer pressure and you're finding it difficult to handle, talk to someone you trust. Don't feel <u>guilty</u> if you've made a mistake or two. Talking to a parent, teacher, or school counselor can help you feel much better and prepare you for the next time you face peer pressure.

Powerful, Positive Peer Pressure

10   Peer pressure is not always a bad thing. For example, positive peer pressure can be used to pressure <u>bullies</u> into acting better toward other kids. If enough kids get together, peers can pressure each other into doing what's right!

———
[1]**pal around with** *pal = friend,* pal around with *means do things together as friends*

2.2 Vocabulary *(10 points)*

Find the underlined word or expression in the indicated paragraph. Choose the meaning that makes sense in the context.

1. <u>convince</u> (¶3) means
   - a. believe
   - b. order
   - c. persuade

2. <u>shoplift</u> (¶3) means
   - a. destroy the merchandise in a store
   - b. move a store to a new location
   - c. take things from a store without paying

3. <u>go along with</u> (¶4) means
   - a. follow
   - b. leave
   - c. thank

© 2009 by Pearson Education, Inc. Duplication for classroom use is permitted.

4. <u>curious</u> (¶4) means

   a. afraid to do something

   b. unable to do something

   c. wanting to know about something

5. <u>tough</u> (¶5) means

   a. difficult   b. simple   c. weak

6. <u>stand firm</u> (¶5) means

   a. not sit down   b. remain strong   c. repeat

7. <u>resist</u> (¶5) means

   a. accept something you don't approve of

   b. continue doing something

   c. try hard not to do something

8. <u>back you up</u> (¶6) means

   a. ask you   b. support you   c. follow you

9. <u>guilty</u> (¶9) means feeling

   a. bad because you have done something wrong

   b. happy about doing something

   c. stupid because you don't understand something

10. <u>bullies</u> (¶10) are people who

   a. frighten and hurt others who are weaker or smaller than they are

   b. help others become accepted in the crowd

   c. teach others new things

2.3 Comprehension *(10 points)*

1. Mark the statements *T* (true) or *F* (false).

1. **T F** According to this article, it's easier to ignore peer pressure if you have the support of a friend.
2. **T F** According to this article, choosing your friends carefully is important.
3. **T F** This article suggests that the reader should look for help from adults if it is needed.
4. **T F** The audience for this article is parents who are worried about peer pressure affecting their children.

2. Answer the questions based on the information in the article.

5. What is one example of positive peer pressure mentioned in this article?

_____

6. What is one example of negative peer pressure mentioned in this article?

_____

© 2009 by Pearson Education, Inc. Duplication for classroom use is permitted.

7. What are two reasons that people give in to peer pressure?

_____

_____

8. What are two things that can help people say "no" to pressure to do something they do not want to do?

_____

_____

© 2009 by Pearson Education, Inc. Duplication for classroom use is permitted.

UNIT 2 BETWEEN TWO WORLDS

PART ONE
REVIEWING

1.1 Paragraph Completion *(10 points)*

Complete the paragraph with items from the list. Use each item only once.

better off	empowering	homelands	make ends meet	obstacles
eager	enables	host countries	newcomers	shortage

    Most people migrate because they will be economically (1) _____ in a different country. In many developed countries there is a(n) (2) _____ of workers; therefore, immigrants can find jobs. In some developing countries even professionals can barely (3) _____ on low salaries, so they leave their (4) _____, creating a brain drain. Many immigrants are determined young people who are (5) _____ to learn new skills, and their flexibility helps them overcome (6) _____. For some women from traditional cultures, starting a new life may be a(n) (7) _____ experience, which (8) _____ them to pursue different careers. It takes time for (9) _____ to integrate into a society, but, hopefully, migration is a rewarding experience for immigrants as well as for people in the (10) _____ that receive them.

1.2 Word Families *(5 points)*

Choose the correct form of the word to complete each sentence.

1. In some host countries, immigrants experience _____.

    a. discrimination   b. discriminate   c. discriminatory

2. Many men _____ to a new country without their wives and children.

    a. migrate   b. migratory   c. immigrant

3. Young people are often more _____ than older people.

    a. resilience   b. resilient   c. resiliently

4. Beatrice is taking a course so she can _____ to work as a health care aide.

    a. qualification   b. qualified   c. qualify

5. In hard times, finding _____ is difficult.

    a. employment   b. employ   c. employed

© 2009 by Pearson Education, Inc. Duplication for classroom use is permitted.

1.3 Matching *(6 points)*

Match the beginning of the sentence on the left with the correct ending on the right. Use each match only once.

_____ 1. Many immigrants leave their homelands to seek

_____ 2. The Bosnian immigrants had a strong work

_____ 3. They pooled

_____ 4. The Bosnians helped transform St. Louis into a thriving

_____ 5. Ethnic

_____ 6. It's a big responsibility to run

a. ethic.

b. conflicts have caused many wars.

c. a business.

d. responsibility for her family.

e. resources to buy homes and businesses.

f. employment abroad.

g. metropolis.

1.4 Writing *(9 points)*

Answer three of the questions. Write two to three sentences for each answer, using information from the readings in the unit.

1. What advantages and disadvantages do young emigrants have?
2. How can migration affect families? Give at least one example.
3. What contributions have the Bosnians made in St. Louis?
4. What are some difficulties that children of immigrants have?

PART TWO
EXPLORING

2.1 Reading

Read the text.

Khadija

Young people of immigrant descent often feel caught between two cultures, and their struggle to find their place may bring them into conflict with not only members of their families and ethnic communities, but also members of their new society.

1   Khadija was born in 1979 in a working class immigrant neighborhood in north Amsterdam[1], the fifth daughter of Moroccan parents. Her father arrived in the Netherlands at the end of the 1960s. Back then, European countries needed Mediterranean workers for jobs the locals <u>rejected</u>. In his homeland, Khadija's father could <u>barely make a living</u> and emigration without his family offered better possibilities.

2   For a long time, Khadija's father lived in crowded rooms packed with other immigrants, away from his family, working full time to send back some money. Ten years passed before he could finally bring his wife and children to live with him. Khadija, the youngest, was born on Dutch soil.

3   *I can't say I'm one thing or the other. I'm a Moroccan Berber who was born in the Netherlands, with Dutch citizenship[2]. I'm both, and that <u>enriches me</u> and troubles me too, all at the same time.*

---

[1]**Amsterdam** *capital of The Netherlands (Holland); the people from The Netherlands are called Dutch.*

[2]**citizenship** *belonging legally to a country and having that country's passport*

© 2009 by Pearson Education, Inc. Duplication for classroom use is permitted.

4   Khadija's father was strict. Sometimes Khadija's mother helped her. For example, when he <u>forbade</u> her to take swimming classes because she would have to appear in a swimsuit in front of boys, her mother secretly took her to the pool.

5   *The teachers invited us to go to meetings and on trips, but he wouldn't let me go. I didn't want my friends to see this man who didn't look like the rest of the parents, who spoke their language badly, who wouldn't let me do things.*

6   Khadija learned that other rules and customs existed outside her front door. She realized she was living in two different worlds, and she had to find a balance between them. Her parents' traditions didn't <u>reflect</u> her own lifestyle, and Dutch society often didn't understand her choices.

7   Her father wouldn't let her go out with boys. That wasn't part of their tradition: boys and girls are supposed to get engaged[3] and then married, but they're not supposed to "go out." Khadija did many things without her father knowing.

8   Khadija was confused. She read the Koran[4] and was very interested in <u>investigating</u> the traditions. One day, at sixteen, she wore a scarf[5] over her head, to see what it felt like. It was a strange experience. She felt as if people didn't see her, or noticed her only because she was different. In those years, Khadija decided to <u>reclaim</u> her beliefs, and now she considers herself a religious person.

9   Three years ago, she started attending philosophy classes, where she is the only Moroccan girl. At first, she didn't like her classmates.

10   *They were "Oh so happy" that I was a Muslim! "We know this is very difficult for you but please don't worry, we'll help you."*

11   Khadija asked them if they knew that philosophy schools had existed in Morocco and the Arab region for centuries.

12   *The one thing I hate is when people try to emancipate[6] me in their own way. They say that we shouldn't live the way we do, that we have to take our scarves off our heads in order to say no to <u>repression</u>. Nobody can tell anybody else how to be free. If we choose to keep our heads covered, it's our decision. I can't accept people telling me how to live my life.*

13   Khadija belongs to a <u>generation</u> of young Muslims who are trying to find a way of being Muslim without turning their backs on the Western world where they grew up; a generation in which girls have acquired new social roles, and often are performing better, academically and professionally, than boys. The daughters of migrants are eager to <u>profit from</u> the opportunities they have in their new society, opportunities that their mothers never had.

---

[3]**get engaged** *decide to get married; engagement is the period between this decision and the actual wedding*

[4]**Koran** *the holy book of Islam as revealed to the prophet Mohammad*

[5]**scarf** (in this case) *head covering worn by Muslim women*

[6]**emancipate** *free, liberate*

2.2 Vocabulary *(10 points)*

Find the underlined word or expression in the indicated paragraph. Choose the meaning that makes sense in the context.

   1. <u>rejected</u> (¶1) means

    a. didn't accept   b. weren't able to do   c. didn't get paid for

© 2009 by Pearson Education, Inc. Duplication for classroom use is permitted.

2. <u>barely make a living</u> (¶1) means

   a. easily make money

   b. have a difficult time making money

   c. have a big house

3. <u>enriches me</u> (¶3) means

   a. makes me fatter

   b. gives me lots of money

   c. is good for me

4. <u>forbade</u> (past tense of *forbid*) (¶4) means

   a. didn't allow   b. encouraged   c. helped

5. <u>reflect</u> (¶6) means

   a. create   b. match   c. think about

6. <u>investigating</u> (¶8) means

   a. changing   b. learning about   c. writing about

7. <u>reclaim</u> (¶8) means

   a. forget about   b. stop   c. take back

8. <u>repression</u> (¶12) means

   a. being controlled, not free

   b. being treated well

   c. being happy and optimistic

9. <u>generation</u> (¶13) means a group of people

   a. attending the same school   b. of similar age   c. of the same religion

10. <u>profit from</u> (¶13) means

   a. benefit from   b. walk away from   c. worry about

2.3 Comprehension *(10 points)*

Mark the statements *T* (true) or *F* (false).

1. **T F** Khadija's father left Morocco with his wife and children.
2. **T F** Khadija is a Dutch citizen.
3. **T F** When she was a child, she liked the fact that her parents were different from Dutch parents.
4. **T F** In traditional Moroccan society, girls go out with boys.
5. **T F** We can infer that Khadija's mother and father did not think the same way.
6. **T F** As a young adult, Khadija became more interested in her Muslim religion and traditions.
7. **T F** Khadija felt good that her university classmates were happy to have a Muslim in class.
8. **T F** We can infer that Khadija's classmates were well-informed about Muslim history and philosophy.
9. **T F** Khadija wanted to find her own type of freedom as a member of two worlds.
10. **T F** Khadija's generation of women, the daughters of Muslim immigrants, are able to advance in ways their mothers could not.

© 2009 by Pearson Education, Inc. Duplication for classroom use is permitted.

UNIT 3 — HIGH TECH—PROS AND CONS

PART ONE
REVIEWING

1.1 Paragraph Completion (10 points)

Complete the paragraph with items from the list. Use each item only once.

accomplish	autonomy	incredible	monitor	simultaneously
addicted	efficiently	keep in touch with	purchases	take for granted

Modern technology has made (1) _____ changes in our lives. We can (2) _____ a lot by using personal computers and doing research on the Internet, and e-mail makes it really easy to (3) _____ friends and family. Computers can also help people with certain disabilities to gain more (4) _____ so they can do some of the things most of us (5) _____. But there are some negative aspects of technology as well. One danger is that people can become (6) _____ to using technology. Many people love multitasking and think they can do several things at the same time, that is (7) _____. However, they are not working as (8) _____ as they think they are; it's really better to do one thing at a time. Another negative aspect of modern technology has to do with the possible invasion of privacy. For example, stores that (9) _____ or keep track of all our (10) _____ are creating an individual profile that can be used in ways we might not expect and might not like. High tech definitely has its pros and cons.

1.2 Word Families (6 points)

Circle the word or expression that is a synonym for the underlined word or expression in the sentence.

1. That's a very <u>complex</u> machine. I don't understand how it works.
   a. complicated   b. incredible   c. unique

2. Pedro has an <u>amazing</u> ability with computers.
   a. boring   b. surprising   c. tragic

3. We are <u>soliciting</u> money to help the victims of the storm.
   a. giving   b. asking for   c. recruiting

4. We're in financial trouble. We have to <u>cut down on</u> spending.
   a. develop   b. trigger   c. reduce

© 2009 by Pearson Education, Inc. Duplication for classroom use is permitted.

5. Many people feel <u>anxious</u> before job interviews.

   a. eager   b. relaxed   c. nervous

6. The <u>recipients</u> of the refurbished computers live in different countries.

   a. people who receive   b. people who give   c. people who make

1.3 Matching *(5 points)*

Match the beginning of the sentence on the left with the correct ending on the right. Use each match only once.

_____ 1. Many stores have surveillance	a. privacy.
_____ 2. I thought we had saturated	b. an increase in many other prices.
_____ 3. Scholarships help defray	c. cameras.
_____ 4. They recruited	d. the costs of education.
_____ 5. The increase in the cost of oil triggered	e. volunteers to clean the beaches.
	f. the market, but there is still demand for our product.

1.4 Writing *(9 points)*

Answer three of the questions. Write two to three sentences for each answer, using information from the readings in the unit.

1. How has technology, such as cell phones and computers, changed our lives for the better? What is at least one danger or problem with it?
2. What has Robert Langford done with computers to make a difference in the lives of people like himself?
3. How has technology changed the field of advertising? Are the changes good or bad? Explain.
4. What do you learn about the man in the story "21" from the profile created by the grocery store computer?

PART TWO

EXPLORING

2.1 Reading

Read the text.

Robots Set to Overhaul Service Industry Jobs

In the next decade, robots will increasingly take over low-level jobs, experts say, displacing human employees.

1   At a mall in Osaka, Japan, lost shoppers can get directions from a robot that looks like something out of *The Jetsons.*[1] In hospitals across the US, robots deliver bed linens and meals to rooms. As a growing number of robots become capable of working with humans,

---

[1]**The Jetsons** *futuristic animated TV series in the 1960s and 1980s about a family who has a robot named Rosie*

© 2009 by Pearson Education, Inc. Duplication for classroom use is permitted.

the service industry may face a problem that is already familiar in the manufacturing sector:[2] robots <u>replacing</u> humans in jobs.

2   "The service sector,[3] which is a gigantic part of the employment picture in the United States, is inevitably going to be a place where you can replace millions of people with robots that work 24/7 for less money," says futurist Marshall Brain.

3   For now, robots such as Robovie, the robot in the Osaka mall that uses cameras and other devices to "understand" human emotions, are <u>more the exception than the rule</u>.

4   "Dealing with humans is a very complex task. It takes us as humans many years to grow up and learn all the social etiquette[4] and cues," says Joel Burdick, a professor of mechanical engineering who specializes in robotics at the California Institute of Technology in Pasadena. It will take time to perfect robots capable of understanding human emotions well enough to please people in service roles, says Dr. Burdick.

5   And, though he expects that robots will have a substantial impact on the service industry, he says that in some cases humans will simply always want to <u>interact with</u> other humans.

6   But robots have already started their march into the service industry. Though they might not look like robots, automated checkout lines at grocery stores or touch-screen check-in kiosks at airports are the <u>tip of</u> the service industry's robotic revolution.

Already at the Hospital

7   In more than 100 hospitals across the U.S., nurses and other employees receive help from robotic "tugs" that pull carts that deliver everything from meals to linens.

8   Once loaded and given a destination, they can drive through crowded hallways, steering around obstacles and stopping if someone unexpectedly steps in front. If something, such as a gurney,[5] is blocking the way, it automatically calls a help desk, where a technician steers around the <u>obstruction</u> or calls the hospital to ask someone to move the roadblock.

9   Like many robotics companies, Aethon, the Pittsburgh-based robotics company that makes the tug, has targeted an industry that has <u>staffing shortages</u>. Instead of <u>eliminating</u> jobs, tugs help nurses and doctors who are <u>already spread thin</u>, says Aldo Zini, president and CEO[6] of Aethon.

10   It's only a matter of time before robots like the tug enter job markets where they will be competing directly with humans. At least one major hotel chain has contacted Aethon to inquire about using the tug for room service. Though the Pittsburgh company has elected to focus on hospitals for now, hotel owners could hire a call center in India to handle all room service orders and e-mail them to the kitchen staff, who would then put them onto a tug for delivery.

11   Though millions of jobs in the service sector are <u>at stake</u>, experts say the change should come gradually enough to create a natural shift in the workforce.

———

[2]**manufacturing sector** *the part of the economy that makes things (products) in factories*

[3]**service sector** *the part of the economy that provides services, not products (e.g. hotels)*

[4]**etiquette** *formal rules for polite behavior*

[5]**gurney** *bed-like table on wheels for moving sick people*

[6]**CEO** *chief executive officer*

© 2009 by Pearson Education, Inc. Duplication for classroom use is permitted.

New Lines of Work

12　In many ways, introducing robots in the service industry might be comparable to the time when personal computers entered the office space, eliminating many basic bookkeeping and accounting jobs, says John Wen, a director of the Center for Automation Technologies and Systems at Rensselaer Polytechnic Institute in Troy, N.Y.

13　"A lot of people that we needed 20 years ago are no longer needed," says Dr. Wen. "However, [the personal computer] has <u>spawned</u> another huge industry—and I see robots doing exactly the same thing."

2.2 Vocabulary *(10 points)*

Find the underlined word or expression in the indicated paragraph. Choose the meaning that makes sense in the context.

1. <u>replacing</u> (¶1) means
   a. being used instead of　　b. growing　　c. making places for

2. <u>more the exception than the rule</u> (¶3) means
   a. less efficient　　b. not common　　c. older

3. <u>interact with</u> (¶5) means
   a. communicate with　　b. hurt　　c. worry about

4. <u>tip of</u> (¶6) means
   a. beginning of　　b. end of　　c. color of

5. <u>obstruction</u> (¶8) is something
   a. good to eat　　b. very dark　　c. blocking the way

6. <u>staffing shortages</u> (¶9) means
   a. having employees who are too short
   b. not having enough employees
   c. having too many employees

7. <u>eliminating</u> (¶9) means
   a. asking for　　b. promising　　c. removing

8. <u>already spread thin</u> (¶9) means
   a. unhealthy　　b. too busy　　c. too fat

9. <u>at stake</u> (¶11) means
   a. available　　b. going to be created　　c. in danger of being lost

10. <u>spawned</u> (¶13) means
    a. destroyed　　b. started　　c. taught

2.3 Comprehension *(10 points)*

Mark the statements *T* (true) or *F* (false).

1. **T F** Factory jobs have already been lost to robots.
2. **T F** Most robots can now understand human emotions and talk to humans.
3. **T F** Joel Burdick believes everyone will prefer to deal with robots rather than humans.
4. **T F** The machines you use to check yourself in at airports are robots.

© 2009 by Pearson Education, Inc. Duplication for classroom use is permitted.

5. **T F** "Tugs" bring things to patients in hospital rooms so employees have time for more important jobs.

6. **T F** According to this article, robots are already commonly used to do a number of jobs in hotels.

7. **T F** Robots in India deliver food to hotel rooms in the United States.

8. **T F** Experts believe the robotic revolution will cause a lot of sudden unemployment.

9. **T F** Many jobs have disappeared over the last couple of decades because of personal computers.

10. **T F** We can infer that Dr. Wen believes that many jobs will be lost due to robots, but a lot of new jobs will be created.

© 2009 by Pearson Education, Inc. Duplication for classroom use is permitted.

© 2009 by Pearson Education, Inc. Duplication for classroom use is permitted.

UNIT 4 LOOKING FOR LOVE

PART ONE
REVIEWING

1.1 Paragraph Completion *(10 points)*

Complete the paragraph with items from the list. Use each item only once.

advice	contemporary	expectations	single	tough
amazed	embarrassing	optimistic	supposed to	turn up

Customs vary from place to place and from generation to generation, but unattached or (1) _____ people around the world are looking for love relationships in their lives. Traditionally in the United States, men were (2) _____ ask girls for dates, call for them at their homes, and pay for the date. However, (3) _____ customs are different. Dating is more casual today, and the rules are less clear, sometimes leading to (4) _____ situations. Today, many people use the Internet to meet others. However, meeting people on the Internet can (5) _____ very strange people, possibly leading to problems. So take the (6) _____ of those who warn you to be very careful when looking for love on the Internet. If you don't like the idea of the Internet, you might be (7) _____ at what you find right next door, like Gary Soto did.

Building a lasting relationship can be (8) _____. Research shows that American college students are more (9) _____ than they should be; it is important to have realistic (10) _____; remember that divorce statistics show that love does not always conquer all.

1.2 Word Families *(6 points)*

Choose the correct form of the word to complete each sentence.

1. Ana looked at me very _____. I wonder what she was thinking.
   a. curiosity   b. curious   c. curiously

2. Stories about how people meet their partners _____ me.
   a. fascination   b. fascinate   c. fascinating

3. It's not a good idea to go out with a _____ person.
   a. marriage   b. marry   c. married

4. We did an OK job on the project. It was _____, but nothing to be really proud of.
   a. satisfaction   b. satisfy   c. satisfactory

5. It takes a great deal of _____ to break up with someone without hurting them.
   a. sensitivity   b. sensitize   c. sensitively

6. Raul is behaving very strangely. I _____ he is hiding something.
   a. suspicion   b. suspect   c. suspicious

1.3 Matching *(5 points)*

Match each of the underlined expressions with its meaning. Use each match only once.

_____ 1. Unrealistic expectations about marriage can <u>set</u> people <u>up for</u> problems in the future.

_____ 2. I'll <u>call for</u> you at 9:00; please be ready.

_____ 3. I <u>couldn't stand</u> the way she treated me.

_____ 4. I didn't know anything about my date, but a friend was able to <u>fill in some of the blanks</u>.

_____ 5. I finally <u>gave in</u> and accepted a date with my brother's best friend.

a. come and get
b. give some information
c. was hurt
d. hated, couldn't tolerate
e. put in a position for
f. agreed

1.4 Writing *(9 points)*

Answer three of the questions. Write two to three sentences for each answer, using information from the readings in the unit.

1. Why is it both good and bad to have high expectations about the future of a love relationship?
2. How is dating today different from dating when Richard Feynman was young?
3. What are some advantages and disadvantages of googling people you might date?
4. Do you think Gary Soto is correct when he says that it is easy to find a spouse (wife or husband)? Explain.

PART TWO

EXPLORING

2.1 Reading

Read the text.

Will You Go Out with Me?

1   Every day I anxiously wait for you to get to class. I can't wait for us to smile at each other and say good morning. Some days, when you arrive only seconds before the lecture begins, I'm incredibly impatient. Instead of reading the *Daily Cal*,[1] I anticipate your footsteps from behind and listen for your voice. Today is one of your late days. But I don't mind, because after a month of desperately wanting to ask you out, today I'm going to.

———
[1]*Daily Cal* college newspaper (Cal *is short for* Californian.)

© 2009 by Pearson Education, Inc. Duplication for classroom use is permitted.

Encourage me, because letting you know I like you seems as <u>risky</u> to me as skydiving[2] into the sea.

2   I know that dating has changed dramatically in the past few years, and for many women, asking men out is not at all <u>daring</u>. But I was raised in a traditional European household. Growing up, I learned that men call, ask, and pay for the date. During my three years at Berkeley, I have learned that isn't always true. My girlfriends <u>insist</u> that it's essential for women to participate more in the dating process. Wonderful. More women are inviting men out, and men say they are <u>delighted</u>, often relieved, that dating no longer solely depends on their willingness and courage to take the first step. Then why am I digging my nails into my hand[3] trying to <u>muster up</u> courage?

3   I keep telling myself to relax, since dating is more casual today. Most of my peers prefer casual dating anyway because it's cheaper and more comfortable. Students have fewer anxiety attacks when they ask somebody to play tennis than when they plan a formal dinner date. They enjoy last-minute "let's make dinner together" dates because they don't have time to <u>agonize</u>.

4   Casual dating also encourages people to form healthy friendships before starting relationships. My roommate and her boyfriend were friends for four months before their chemistries clicked.[4] They went to movies and meals and often got together with mutual friends. They took turns paying the dinner check. "He was like a girlfriend," my roommate once laughed—blushing.[5]

5   Who pays for it? My past dates have taught me some things: You don't know if I'll get the wrong idea if you treat me for dinner,[6] and I don't know if I'll <u>offend</u> you by insisting on paying for myself. John took out his wallet on our first date before I could suggest we go Dutch.[7] During our after-dinner walk he told me he was interested in dating me <u>on a steady basis</u>. After I explained I was more interested in a friendship, he told me he would have understood had I paid for my dinner.

6   Larry, on the other hand, blushed when I offered to pay for my meal on our first date. Hesitant, I asked politely, "How much do I owe you?" To Larry, my gesture was a <u>suggestion of rejection</u>.

7   Both men and women are <u>confused</u> about who should ask whom out and who should pay. While I value my femininity, love gentlemen, and delight in a traditional formal date, I also believe in equality. I am grateful for casual dating because it has improved my social life immensely by making me an active participant in the process. Now I not only can receive roses but can also give them.

8   Sliding into his desk, he taps my shoulder and says, "Hi, Laura, what's up?"

9   "Good morning," I answer with nervous chills. "Hey, how would you like to have lunch after class on Friday?"

10   "You mean after the midterm?" he says encouragingly. "I'd love to go to lunch with you."

11   "We have a date," I smile.

---

[2]**skydiving** *jumping from an airplane using a parachute*

[3]**digging my nails into my hand** *pushing her fingernails into her hand because she is so nervous*

[4]**chemistries clicked** *had romantic feelings for each other*

[5]**blushing** *turning red from embarrassment*

[6]**treat me for dinner** *pay for the meal*

[7]**go Dutch** *each person pays his/her own bill*

© 2009 by Pearson Education, Inc. Duplication for classroom use is permitted.

2.2 Vocabulary *(10 points)*

Find the underlined word or expression in the indicated paragraph. Choose the meaning that makes sense in the context.

1. risky (¶1) means
   a. minor   b. old-fashioned   c. dangerous

2. daring (¶2) means
   a. neither false nor true   b. courageous or bold   c. active and healthy

3. insist (¶2) means
   a. have difficulty remembering something
   b. forget over and over again
   c. say firmly that something is true

4. delighted (¶2) means
   a. not heavy   b. very happy   c. sad

5. muster up (¶2) means
   a. find   b. forget   c. clean

6. agonize (¶3) means
   a. agree with someone
   b. read the assignment
   c. think hard or worry about something

7. offend (¶5) means
   a. hurt someone's feelings   b. take someone's money   c. tell the truth

8. on a steady basis (¶5) means
   a. carefully   b. regularly   c. unfortunately

9. suggestion of rejection (¶6) means
   a. suggestion that she was happy
   b. suggestion that she didn't like him
   c. suggestion that she was intelligent

10. confused (¶7) means
    a. certain   b. comfortable   c. unable to understand

2.3 Comprehension *(10 points)*

1. Mark the statements *T* (true) or *F* (false).

1. **T F** The writer wants to ask a guy in her apartment building out on a date
2. **T F** The writer grew up with the idea that women can ask men out on dates.
3. **T F** The writer's girlfriends ask men out on dates.
4. **T F** The writer's roommate fell in love with her boyfriend in the first week.
5. **T F** In casual dating, either men or women can ask someone out on a date.
6. **T F** Both men and women can be unclear on who pays for a date.
7. **T F** The writer overcame her nervousness and asked the man out.

2. What are three advantages to casual dating mentioned in the reading?

_____

_____

_____

© 2009 by Pearson Education, Inc. Duplication for classroom use is permitted.

UNIT 5 THE ENTERPRISING SPIRIT

© 2009 by Pearson Education, Inc. Duplication for classroom use is permitted.

PART ONE
REVIEWING

1.1 Paragraph Completion *(10 points)*

Complete the paragraphs with items from the list. Use each item only once.

certified	eliminate	eventually	left over	microlending
dignified	established	launch	living wage	raise

Before entrepreneurs (1) _____ a business, they have to (2) _____ capital. When people risk their money by investing in a business, they hope that the business will (3) _____ be successful and make a profit: that is, have money (4) _____ after paying expenses.

Not everyone has money to start even a small business, especially in poorer countries. In 2004 Matt Flannery (5) _____ a website (kiva.org) to fund entrepreneurs in developing countries around the world through (6) _____. According to Flannery, lending money for startup or operating capital is a more (7) _____ way of helping people than giving them money. The Fair Trade movement also helps poorer people become entrepreneurs. Fair Trade cooperatives buy what they need as a group and (8) _____ middlemen. Products that are (9) _____ as Fair Trade sell for slightly higher prices so producers can earn a(n) (10) _____.

1.2 Word Families *(5 points)*

Choose the correct form of the word to complete each sentence.

1. In the free enterprise system, businesses _____ for customers.
   a. competition   b. compete   c. competitive

2. Building a strong and profitable business requires the _____ of time and energy in addition to money.
   a. investment   b. investor   c. invest

3. Entrepreneurs are often true _____; they bring something new into existence.
   a. innovations   b. innovators   c. innovative

4. When the cooperative bought a tractor, they _____ certain aspects of growing coffee.
   a. mechanized   b. mechanical   c. mechanically

5. Students help out on the farm _____; they don't get paid.
   a. volunteer   b. voluntary   c. voluntarily

1.3 Matching *(6 points)*

Match the beginning of the sentence on the left with the correct ending on the right. Use each match only once.

_____ 1. It's easy to post
_____ 2. Fair
_____ 3. I'd rather renovate
_____ 4. It's risky to undertake
_____ 5. It takes imagination to come up with
_____ 6. People and businesses in the developed world often take technology

a. a business venture.
b. for granted.
c. a living wage.
d. information on the Internet.
e. trade coffee is usually a little more expensive.
f. innovative ideas.
g. an old building than destroy it.

1.4 Writing *(9 points)*

Answer three of the questions. Write two to three sentences for each answer, using information from the readings in the unit.

1. What does an entrepreneur do? Do you think you would like to be one? Explain.
2. What is free enterprise, and why is it good for consumers?
3. Why was Flannery interested in helping people in developing countries?
4. What are cooperatives, and how do they benefit entrepreneurs in the Fair Trade movement?

PART TWO

EXPLORING

2.1 Reading

Read the text.

A Frightening Deadline

American history is rich with tales of legendary entrepreneurs who disregarded the "experts" and risked all to chase their dreams. But for every well-known Tom Edison or Bill Gates there are unsung thousands whose vision and perseverance have won them success.

1 On a fall night in 1989, Scott McGregor, 45, was working at his home computer in Walnut Creek, Calif. Lifting tired eyes from the screen, he saw his teenage twin sons Chris and Travis with his wife Diane in the kitchen beyond. The three were stacking coins to buy milk.

2 Stricken with guilt, McGregor walked into the kitchen. "I can't do this to you anymore," he said. "I'll go out tomorrow and get a job."

3 "You can't quit now, Dad," Travis protested. Added Chris: "You're almost there!"

4 Two years earlier McGregor had quit a secure position as a consultant[1] to pursue an idea. He'd worked with a company that rented fold-up cellular phones to business travelers at airports and hotels. But the phones weren't set up to produce itemized bills,[2] and some

---

[1] **consultant** *person with experience whose job is to advise other people in that area*

[2] **itemized bill** *in this case a list of individual phone calls and their cost*

© 2009 by Pearson Education, Inc. Duplication for classroom use is permitted.

corporations wouldn't <u>reimburse</u> their employees without one. Needed was a computer chip, built into the phones, that would make a billing record of each call.

5   McGregor knew his idea was a sure winner. With his family's support he began approaching investors. But the venture seemed to go nowhere.

6   He reached <u>rock bottom</u> one Friday in March 1990 when a sheriff's deputy[3] rapped on the McGregors' door. If the rent wasn't paid by Monday, they'd be on the street.

7   Desperate, McGregor worked all weekend calling investors. At eleven o'clock on Sunday night, one finally promised to send a check.

8   Remembering the eviction notice,[4] McGregor asked, "Could you make that an electronic bank transfer?"[5]

9   With the money, McGregor paid bills and hired a consulting engineer. But after several months the engineer said the system McGregor wanted was impossible. "Keep trying," McGregor told him.

10   By May 1991 the family was again facing financial disaster. McGregor made a call to BellSouth, the telecommunications giant. "Can you <u>demonstrate a prototype</u> by June 24?" an executive asked.

11   McGregor remembered the naysaying engineer and pictured his own workbench <u>strewn with failed components</u>. "You bet,"[6] he said, hoping his voice sounded <u>confident</u>.

12   He immediately called his oldest son, Greg, who was majoring in computer science in college, and described the enormous challenge.

13   Greg began working up to 18 hours a day to create the automated circuit that had defeated the experts. It was a tough problem: Somehow he had to create a billing system to <u>integrate</u> the credit-card accounting and timekeeping software with a system that could track where the phone was and where the call was going—all on a single, fingernail-size chip. On June 23, Scott and Greg flew to Atlanta with their unproven solution.

14   After Scott introduced his 22-year-old son to the BellSouth executives, Greg handed the prototype phone to one. "Ma'am," he said, "go ahead." She slid a credit card through the phone and made a call. It went through <u>without a hitch</u>. Then Greg handed a perfect billing printout to the BellSouth team.

15   Today the McGregor family firm, Telemac Cellular Corp., is an industry leader worth millions of dollars. Looking back on the days when <u>defeat</u> seemed certain, Scott McGregor speaks of his wife and children with intense pride. "We've been tested," he says. "This family is strong."

---

[3]**sheriff's deputy** *an officer of the law, similar to a police officer*

[4]**eviction notice** *legal document saying a renter must leave a house or apartment*

[5]**electronic bank transfer** *way to move money so that it can be used immediately*

[6]**You bet** *Yes, of course.*

2.2 Vocabulary *(10 points)*

Find the underlined word or expression in the indicated paragraph. Choose the meaning that makes sense in the context.

1. <u>stricken with guilt</u> (¶2) means

    a. feeling good   b. feeling bad   c. feeling lucky

2. <u>pursue</u> (¶4) means

    a. follow   b. paint   c. waste

© 2009 by Pearson Education, Inc. Duplication for classroom use is permitted.

3. <u>reimburse</u> (¶4) means

    a. offer a job to   b. order lunch for   c. pay money back to someone

4. <u>rock bottom</u> (¶6) means

    a. the best situation   b. a safe situation   c. the worst situation

5. <u>demonstrate a prototype</u> (¶10) means

    a. call us tomorrow   b. buy some parts   c. show an example

6. <u>strewn with failed components</u> (¶11) means

    a. covered with parts that didn't work

    b. covered with torn paper

    c. covered with expensive food

7. <u>confident</u> (¶11) means

    a. laughing, funny   b. positive, sure   c. negative, afraid

8. <u>integrate</u> (¶13) means

    a. eliminate   b. destroy   c. put together

9. <u>without a hitch</u> (¶14) means

    a. with lots of problems   b. with no problems   c. with some problems

10. <u>defeat</u> (¶15) means

    a. success   b. failure   c. winning

2.3 Comprehension *(10 points)*

1. Mark the statements *T* (true) or *F* (false).

1. **T F** Scott McGregor left his job at a company that rented cellular phones in airports and hotels because he didn't like it.
2. **T F** Scott McGregor felt bad about the financial pressure put on his family, but they didn't want him to give up.
3. **T F** McGregor saw a need for a computer chip that would print out an itemized bill of every call made.
4. **T F** McGregor finally found someone to invest more money in the business.
5. **T F** The engineer McGregor hired was successful.
6. **T F** The chip that McGregor's son invented combined software for itemized billing and timekeeping records.
7. **T F** McGregor was completely honest with Bell South.

2. Check all ideas that complete the sentence correctly. (3 points)

This story shows that

    a. _____ entrepreneurs sometimes have to take risks.

    b. _____ success in business sometimes comes easily.

    c. _____ an entrepreneur needs capital and investors to start a business.

    d. _____ a successful business meets a need.

    e. _____ an entrepreneur recognizes an opportunity for a business that others may not see.

    f. _____ you have a better chance of success if you work alone.

© 2009 by Pearson Education, Inc. Duplication for classroom use is permitted.

UNIT 6 FINDING YOUR WAY

PART ONE
REVIEWING

1.1 Paragraph Completion (10 points)

Complete the paragraphs with items from the list. Use each item only once.

came up with	confident	insight	passion	profile
compatible	expertise	naïve	potential	pursue

In order to find your way in life, you first must know who you are. You need
(1) _____ into your (2) _____ of intelligences and your
styles of learning and thinking. It is important to (3) _____ a career that is
(4) _____ with your abilities and style; it should be something you do well
and enjoy. You'll be really lucky if you find your (5) _____: what you really
love to do, as Maria Shriver did.

When Shriver started her first job at a television station, she was (6) _____
and had a lot to learn, but she was (7) _____ that she could succeed. She
started at the bottom, did everything she was assigned, and even (8) _____
other things to do.

When you have found the right career, it is easier to remain enthusiastic and reach your
full (9) _____. Remember that no one has (10) _____ in
everything, so don't be discouraged if it takes time to find the career that is the best fit
for you.

1.2 Word Families (5 points)

Choose the correct form of the word to complete each sentence.

1. Be sure all the information on your job application is _____.
   a. accuracy   b. accurate   c. accurately

2. I don't _____ to keep this job forever.
   a. intend   b. intentional   c. intentionally

3. We had to make a major _____ in the schedule.
   a. modification   b. modify   c. modified

4. There's only one _____ answer to this question.
   a. logic   b. logician   c. logical

© 2009 by Pearson Education, Inc. Duplication for classroom use is permitted.

5. It was very _____ of my academic advisor to realize I was majoring in the wrong field.

    a. perception   b. perceive   c. perceptive

1.3 Multiple Choice *(6 points)*

Circle the word or expression that is a synonym for the underlined word or expression in the sentence.

1. My sister went to a <u>prestigious</u> college.

    a. awful   b. respected   c. rural

2. Mary <u>lacks</u> the ability to understand her own motivations.

    a. doesn't have   b. doesn't want   c. likes

3. Take time to <u>reflect on</u> what is important in your life.

    a. contend with   b. diminish   c. think about

4. Once you are an adult, you <u>are in charge of</u> your life.

    a. should be careful of

    b. are responsible for

    c. start at the bottom of

5. The women's tennis team did an <u>outstanding</u> job in the tournament.

    a. apparent   b. excellent   c. tough

6. I'm <u>mediocre</u> in sports.

    a. excellent   b. not good, not bad   c. capable, talented

1.4 Writing *(9 points)*

Answer three of the questions. Write two to three sentences for each answer, using information from the readings in the unit.

1. What are your two strongest intelligences, and how do you plan to use them?
2. What are styles of thinking and learning? Illustrate with reference to Alex, Bill, and/or Curt.
3. What advice does Maria Shriver give people who are starting their careers?
4. Why do you think that college students don't have the same enthusiasm and self-confidence of kindergartners?

© 2009 by Pearson Education, Inc. Duplication for classroom use is permitted.

EXPLORING

2.1 Reading

Read the text.

What Is Intelligence, Anyway?

1   What is intelligence, anyway? When I was in the army, I received the kind of aptitude test[1] that all soldiers took and, against a normal of 100, scored 160. No one at the base had ever seen a <u>figure</u> like that, and for two hours they <u>made a big fuss over me</u>. (It didn't mean anything. The next day I was still a buck private[2] with KP—kitchen police[3]—as my highest duty.)

2   All my life I've been registering scores like that, so that I have the <u>complacent</u> feeling that I'm highly intelligent, and I expect other people to think so, too. Actually, though, don't such scores simply mean that I am very good at answering the type of academic questions that are considered worthy of answers by people who make up the intelligence tests—people with intellectual <u>bents</u> similar to mine?

3   For instance, I had an auto repairman once, who, on these intelligence tests, could not possibly have scored more than 80, by my estimate. I always took it for granted that I was far more intelligent than he was. Yet, when anything went wrong with my car I <u>hastened</u> to him with it, watched him anxiously as he explored its <u>vitals</u>, and listened to <u>his pronouncements</u> as though they were divine oracles[4]—and he always fixed my car.

4   Well, then, suppose my auto repairman <u>devised</u> questions for an intelligence test. Or suppose a carpenter did, or a farmer, or, indeed, almost anyone but an academician. By every one of those tests, I'd prove myself a <u>moron</u>. And, I'd be a moron, too. In a world where I could not use my academic training and my verbal talents but had to do something intricate or hard, working with my hands, I would do poorly. My intelligence, then, is not absolute but is a function of the society I live in and of the fact that a small subsection of that society has managed to foist itself on the rest as an arbiter of such matters.[5]

5   Consider my auto repairman, again. He had a habit of telling me jokes whenever he saw me. One time he raised his head from under the automobile hood to say: "Doc, a deaf-and-mute[6] guy went into a hardware store to ask for some nails. He put two fingers together on the counter and made hammering motions with the other hand. The clerk brought him a hammer. He shook his head and pointed to the two fingers he was hammering. The clerk brought him nails. He picked out the sizes he wanted, and left. Well, doc, the next guy who came in was a blind man. He wanted scissors. How do you suppose he asked for them?"

6   Indulgently, I lifted my right hand and made scissoring motions with my first two fingers. Whereupon my auto-repair man laughed <u>raucously</u> and said, "Why, you <u>dumb jerk</u>, he used his voice and asked for them." Then he said <u>smugly</u>, "I've been trying that on all my

---

[1]**aptitude test** *a test to reveal abilities*

[2]**buck private** *soldier with the lowest rank*

[3]**KP—kitchen police** *kitchen workers who help cook and clean up*

[4]**divine oracles** *words coming from a god*

[5]**a small subsection of that society has managed to foist itself on the rest as an arbiter of such matters** *a small group of people (test makers) have convinced everyone else that they (the test makers) know how to decide who is smart*

[6]**deaf-and-mute** *unable to hear and speak*

© 2009 by Pearson Education, Inc. Duplication for classroom use is permitted.

customers today." "Did you catch many?" I asked. "Quite a few," he said, "but I knew for sure I'd catch you." "Why is that?" I asked. "Because you're so goddamned educated, doc, I knew you couldn't be very smart."

7   And I have an uneasy feeling he had something there.

2.2 Vocabulary *(12 points)*

Find the underlined word or expression in the indicated paragraph. Choose the meaning that makes sense in the context.

1. figure (¶1) means
    a. face   b. number   c. shape

2. made a big fuss over me (¶1) means
    a. decided to send me to college
    b. gave me a better job
    c. paid a lot of attention to me

3. complacent (¶2) means
    a. satisfied   b. sick   c. worried

4. bents (¶2) means
    a. bones   b. muscles   c. natural abilities

5. hastened (¶3) means
    a. hurried   b. phoned   c. walked

6. vitals (¶3) means
    a. important parts   b. tires   c. windows

7. his pronouncements (¶3) means
    a. what he eats   b. what he had to say c. his health problems

8. devised (¶4) means
    a. wrote   b. refused   c. reported

9. moron (¶4) means
    a. sleepy person   b. rich person   c. stupid person

10. raucously (¶6) means
    a. loudly   b. sadly   c. seriously

11. dumb jerk (¶6) means
    a. intelligent guy   b. handsome guy   c. stupid guy

12. smugly (¶6) means
    a. angrily   b. sure of himself   c. often

2.3 Comprehension *(8 points)*

1. Mark the statements *T* (true) or *F* (false).

1. **T F** Asimov suggests he scored high on the intelligence test because he has the abilities the test writers consider important for intelligence.
2. **T F** Asimov thinks that his auto repairman (mechanic) has the same type of intelligence as he does.

© 2009 by Pearson Education, Inc. Duplication for classroom use is permitted.

3. **T F** Asimov thinks he would probably be a good mechanic.
4. **T F** The joke that the mechanic tells is supposed to trick people and make them look kind of stupid.
5. **T F** The mechanic was not surprised that Asimov answered his question incorrectly.
6. **T F** We can infer that the intelligence to answer the joke correctly is based on book learning.
7. **T F** In the end Asimov believes that his mechanic may be right: He (Asimov) is a bit dumb, at least in some areas.

2. Answer the question. *(3 points)*

How does this piece of writing relate to Gardner's theory of multiple intelligences?

_____

_____

© 2009 by Pearson Education, Inc. Duplication for classroom use is permitted.

Unit Tests
Answer Key

Note that answers for the Writing sections of the tests are only suggestions to give teachers an idea of what to look for in students' answers. It is up to teachers to determine how they evaluate use of vocabulary, writing style, and grammatical accuracy. Furthermore, students will undoubtedly come up with other good answers, perhaps based on class discussion, which certainly should be accepted.

UNIT 1 — GROWING UP

PART ONE

1.1 Paragraph Completion

1. influence
2. concerned about
3. teased
4. bother
5. adolescence
6. alienated
7. look out for
8. find out
9. capable of
10. contented

1.2 Word Families

1.	b	3.	a	5.	c
2.	c	4.	a		

1.3 Matching

1.	c	3.	a	5.	f
2.	e	4.	g	6.	d

1.4 Writing

Answers will vary. Suggested answers:

1. His father never put pressure on him to do well in things like sports. However, Powell felt very bad if he disappointed his father.
2. According to research, peers have a much greater influence on adolescents than parents. Peers influence how students do in school and whether or not they use drugs and alcohol. Parents have little influence in these areas but more of an influence on educational goals.
3. Angie says that parents should teach their children to accept people who are different and that it's OK to be friends with people who are different. They should realize that a disabled person needs friends and love just like anyone else.
4. When you teach your child something like how to ride a bicycle, you have to support or help them in the beginning. At some point, you have to let them go even if they fall or get hurt. You cannot always be there to protect the child. In other words, the poem shows that parents have to let their children grow up and become independent.

PART TWO

2.2 Vocabulary

1.	c	5.	a	9.	a
2.	c	6.	b	10.	a
3.	a	7.	c		
4.	c	8.	b		

2.3 Comprehension

1. T (¶6)
2. T (¶7, ¶6)
3. T (¶9)
4. F advice refers to experience of young people; no reference to 'your son/daughter/children'

5. *One of the following:*
    a classmate who teaches you an easy way to remember the planets;
    someone on the soccer team who teaches you a trick with the ball;
    you may admire someone and try to be more like that person;
    you might get excited about a favorite book and now everyone's reading it (¶2)
6. *One of the following:*
    kids at school might try to get you to cut class;
    a soccer friend might want you to be mean to another player;
    a kid in the neighborhood might want you to shoplift with him (¶3)

7. *Students should provide two of the following:* (¶4)
    People give in to peer pressure because they want to be liked and to fit in
    They might be curious about trying something new.
    They may be afraid other kids will make fun of them if they don't go along with the group.
8. It helps to have at least one ally who backs you up in resisting peer pressure. (¶6)
    You should pay attention to your own feelings and beliefs about what is right and wrong. Inferred (¶6, 8)

UNIT 2 BETWEEN TWO WORLDS

PART ONE

1.1 Paragraph Completion

1. better off
2. shortage
3. make ends meet
4. homeland
5. eager
6. obstacles
7. empowering
8. enables
9. newcomers
10. host countries

1.2 Word Families

1. a	3. b	5. a
2. a	4. c	

1.3 Matching

1. f	3. e	5. b
2. a	4. g	6. c

1.4 Writing

Answers will vary. Suggested answers:

1. Young emigrants are usually resilient, resourceful, persevering and determined. They are eager to learn new skills. But when they migrate alone, they leave their support system of family and friends, and this might affect their sense of identity and how comfortable they feel in their new country.
2. Migration can separate families, for example, when young people migrate alone. Another example is the separation of Rajini and her husband. She didn't leave India, but her husband did, and they only see each other every two and a half years.
3. Bosnians have changed the Bevo neighborhood in St. Louis from a depressed area to a thriving area. They have a good work ethic, so they are good employees. Some have started their own businesses, and families have pooled their resources to buy houses. (You may also decide to accept examples from personal experience.)

4. Children, like Patricia Tumang, can feel like outsiders in both cultures. They do not feel part of their parents' culture, especially if they do not know the language. They don't feel just like the children in the country they live in either. For example, Tumang's classmates thought she ate weird food like chicken adobo. Also, aspects of American culture, such as Barbie dolls and cartoons on TV, did not really resonate with her.

2.2 Vocabulary

1.	a	5.	b	9.	b
2.	b	6.	b	10.	a
3.	c	7.	c		
4.	a	8.	a		

2.3 Comprehension

1.	F (¶1,2)	6.	T (¶8)
2.	T (¶3)	7.	F (¶9–11)
3.	F (¶5)	8.	F (¶11)
4.	F (¶7)	9.	T (¶12,13)
5.	T (¶4)	10.	T (¶13)

UNIT 3 HIGH TECH—PROS AND CONS

PART ONE

1.1 Paragraph Completion

1. incredible
2. accomplish
3. keep in touch with
4. autonomy
5. take for granted
6. addicted
7. simultaneously
8. efficiently
9. monitor
10. purchases

1.2 Word Families

1.	a	3.	b	5.	c
2.	b	4.	c	6.	a

1.3 Matching

1.	c	3.	d	5.	b
2.	f	4.	e		

1.4 Writing

Answers will vary. Suggested answers:

1. Cell phones and computers have changed our lives by making communication much faster and easier. We can e-mail, IM, send text messages, create social networking pages—lots of things that keep us in contact with as many people as we want. We can also use the Internet to do research, get news, watch movies, etc. One danger is that when we try to multitask, we work less efficiently. Another danger is that spending so much time online can take away from face-to-face contact with our friends, and we may not get out and do other things.

2. Robert Langford, who has been blind since he was 15, coordinates a program that collects donated computers and refurbishes them for visually-impaired people. Volunteers put new software in them, voice-synthesized software for the totally blind and text-enlarging software for the partially blind. The recipients pay only $100 to help cover the costs involved in shipping the computers to them.

3. Technology makes it possible for marketers to personalize the ads they direct to individuals. For example, stores can keep a profile based on the things you typically buy and then direct ads to you based on the things they know you might use. Cameras in stores also observe you and watch what you look at; then they can target ads based on what you show an interest in. Some people think this is an invasion of privacy.

4. He doesn't do much cooking for himself; he buys prepared foods (roasted chicken legs) and Meals for One. He probably doesn't do much cleaning either because he doesn't buy cleaning products very often. His cat must have died or disappeared because he no longer buys cat food. He has tried (but failed) to cut down on fattening things like pastries and croissants. He never goes on long trips (he has never left the neighborhood for more than a week). He sometimes buys cigars. He watches his health in some ways (he buys fat-free yogurt, decaf coffee), and he takes vitamins.

2.2 Vocabulary

1. a	5. c	9. c
2. b	6. b	10. b
3. a	7. c	
4. a	8. b	

2.3 Comprehension

1. T (¶1)
2. F (¶3–4)
3. F (¶5)
4. T (¶6)
5. T (¶7–9)
6. F (¶10)
7. F (¶10)
8. F (¶11)
9. T (¶12)
10. T (¶13

UNIT 4

LOOKING FOR LOVE

1.1 Paragraph Completion

1. single
2. supposed to
3. contemporary
4. embarrassing
5. turn up
6. advice
7. amazed
8. tough
9. optimistic
10. expectations

1.2 Word Families

1. c	3. c	5. a
2. b	4. c	6. b

1.3 Matching

1. e	3. d	5. f
2. a	4. b	

1.4. Writing

Answers will vary. Suggested answers:

1. The researchers in "Students Think Love Conquers All" think positive expectations make people work harder, which is good—up to a point. After that point such high expectations, such as thinking your relationship will always continue to get better and better, are simply unrealistic. It is also unrealistic to assume your relationship should be better than other people's.

2. In the 1930s (40s and 50s) dating was more formal and traditional. For example, boys asked girls out and called for them at their houses. Both boys and girls got

dressed up for a date. Now dating is less formal. People meet people through the Internet and use the Internet to find out about the people they date.

3. Googling a date can give you information about the person, which might tell you whether or not you want to go out with them. On the other hand, a first date can be a little awkward if you already have information about the person; then you have to pretend you don't know much about them. You might find out the person is not telling you the truth about himself/herself, which can serve as a useful warning. Also, if you can google other people, they can certainly google you, and you might not like that.

4. The way Soto met his neighbor, Carolyn, seems pretty realistic. It's also realistic that people are attracted to each other very quickly. However, the idea that a two- or three-week courtship is enough to really know if you should marry a person is more questionable.

2.2 Vocabulary

1.	c	5.	a	9.	b
2.	b	6.	c	10.	c
3.	c	7.	a		
4.	b	8.	b		

2.3 Comprehension

Part 1

1. F (¶1)
2. F (¶2)
3. T (¶2–3)
4. F (¶4)
5. T (¶2)
6. T (¶5–6)
7. T (¶9)

Part 2

Students should provide 3 of the following 4 reasons:

—It's cheaper.

—It's more comfortable.

—There's less anxiety and agonizing.

—It's good to form healthy friendships before starting romantic relationships.

UNIT 5 THE ENTERPRISING SPIRIT

PART ONE

1.1 Paragraph Completion

1. launch
2. raise
3. eventually
4. left over
5. established
6. microlending
7. dignified
8. eliminate
9. certified
10. living wage

1.2 Word Families

1.	b	3.	b	5.	c
2.	a	4.	a		

1.3 Matching

1.	d	3.	g	5.	f
2.	e	4.	a	6.	b

1.4 Writing

Answers will vary. Suggested answers:

1. Entrepreneurs start their own businesses. They add value to resources by providing a product or a service. They take a risk, but they own the profit, from their business. They can reinvest the profit in the business or they can use the money to pay themselves. (Response to the second question is personal.)

2. In a free enterprise system anyone is free to start a business. Consumers benefit because competition forces producers to keep quality high and prices as low as possible. If a business doesn't give good service, doesn't sell good products, or charges too much, it will lose customers to the competition.

3. Flannery grew up with an interest in doing something about poverty. His family always donated money to help poor children through their church. He sees microlending as another way to lift people out of poverty. He knows that a small loan can make it possible for a business in a developing country to succeed.

4. A cooperative is a business owned equally by the workers. In the Fair Trade movement, the co-op might be a group of farmers or artisans. By working together, co-op members can do some of the things that are typically done by intermediaries. For example, they can pool their resources to buy a truck to transport their goods to a port instead of having an intermediary do that job.

2.2 Vocabulary

1. b	5. c	9. b
2. a	6. a	10. b
3. c	7. b	
4. c	8. c	

2.3 Comprehension

Part 1

1. F (¶4)	5. F (¶9)
2. T (¶1–3)	6. T (¶13)
3. T (¶4)	7. F (¶10–11, 13)
4. T (¶7)	

Part 2

Items a, b, c, d, e should be checked. Give ½ point for each item that is correctly checked or correctly left blank (for a total of 3 points).

PART ONE

1.1 Paragraph Completion

1. insight
2. profile
3. pursue
4. compatible
5. passion
6. naïve
7. confident
8. came up with
9. potential
10. expertise

1.2 Word Families

1. b		3. a		5. c	
2. a		4. c			

1.3 Multiple Choice

1. b		3. c		5. b	
2. a		4. b		6. b	

1.4 Writing

Answers will vary. Suggested answers:

1. *This question entails personal responses.*
2. Styles of thinking and learning are not the same as intelligence; they refer to the ways we use our abilities. Alex, Bill, and Curt were all intelligent, but their styles were different. Alex liked to work in a structured way because he was good at following directions but not particularly creative. He did well as a contracts lawyer. Bill did not like structure; he preferred to think for himself and did well as a research scientist. Curt liked to evaluate people and things, so he was successful as a psychotherapist.
3. Maria Shriver tells college graduates who are starting their careers that they should be willing to start at the bottom; they should not think any job is beneath them. Starting at the bottom is the best way to learn, and it builds character. Her first job, a glorified internship, was at a TV news station where she worked really hard doing all sorts of jobs. Based on that experience, she tells young people that it takes time to get to the top, but that is a good thing because by the time you get there, you will have learned what you need to know to do the job well.
4. As people grow up they become more limited in what they feel confident doing. There are probably a lot of reasons why this happens, but one of them is certainly that we cannot be good at everything. In addition, adults probably have higher standards for what it means to do something well. They may have been criticized for not singing well, for example, which made them lose their confidence.

PART TWO

2.2 Vocabulary

1. b		5. a		9. c	
2. c		6. a		10. a	
3. a		7. b		11. c	
4. c		8. a		12. b	

2.3 Comprehension

Part 1
1. T (¶2)
2. F (¶3)
3. F (¶4)
4. T (¶5–6)
5. T (¶6)
6. F (¶6)
7. T (¶7, 4)

Part 2
Asimov realizes he has certain types of intelligence (probably verbal, logical mathematical), but not others. The mechanic probably relies more on different intelligences (probably bodily-kinesthetic and spatial).

Notes

Notes

Notes

World of Reading 1
Student Book   0-13-600244-7   978-0-13-600244-4
Teacher's Manual with Tests   0-13-600210-2   978-0-13-600210-9

World of Reading 2
Student Book   0-13-600211-0   978-0-13-600211-6
Teacher's Manual with Tests   0-13-600212-9   978-0-13-600212-3

World of Reading 3
Student Book   0-13-600214-5   978-0-13-600214-7
Teacher's Manual with Tests   0-13-600215-3   978-0-13-600215-4

PEARSON
Longman

www.pearsonlongman.com

ISBN-13: 978-0-13-600212-3
ISBN-10:   0-13-600212-9

EAN

9 780136 002123

90000 >

Exploring Research

NINTH EDITION

Neil J. Salkind

Pearson